Finding Myself in Salvaged Layers

How Encaustic Art Healed Me

Sharon Mirtaheri

DEDICATION

To Professor Nancy Dahlstrom, whose nurturing changed the direction of my life.

And, to Denny Arrant—now deceased—who first believed in my talent as an artist.

With a grateful heart I would like to acknowledge Tonia Jenny for her stellar work in co-birthing this book. Without her it would not be possible.

And in gratitude to my soul-mate, best friend, husband, Koran Dei-Anang for his unrelenting support of all my efforts no matter what they are.

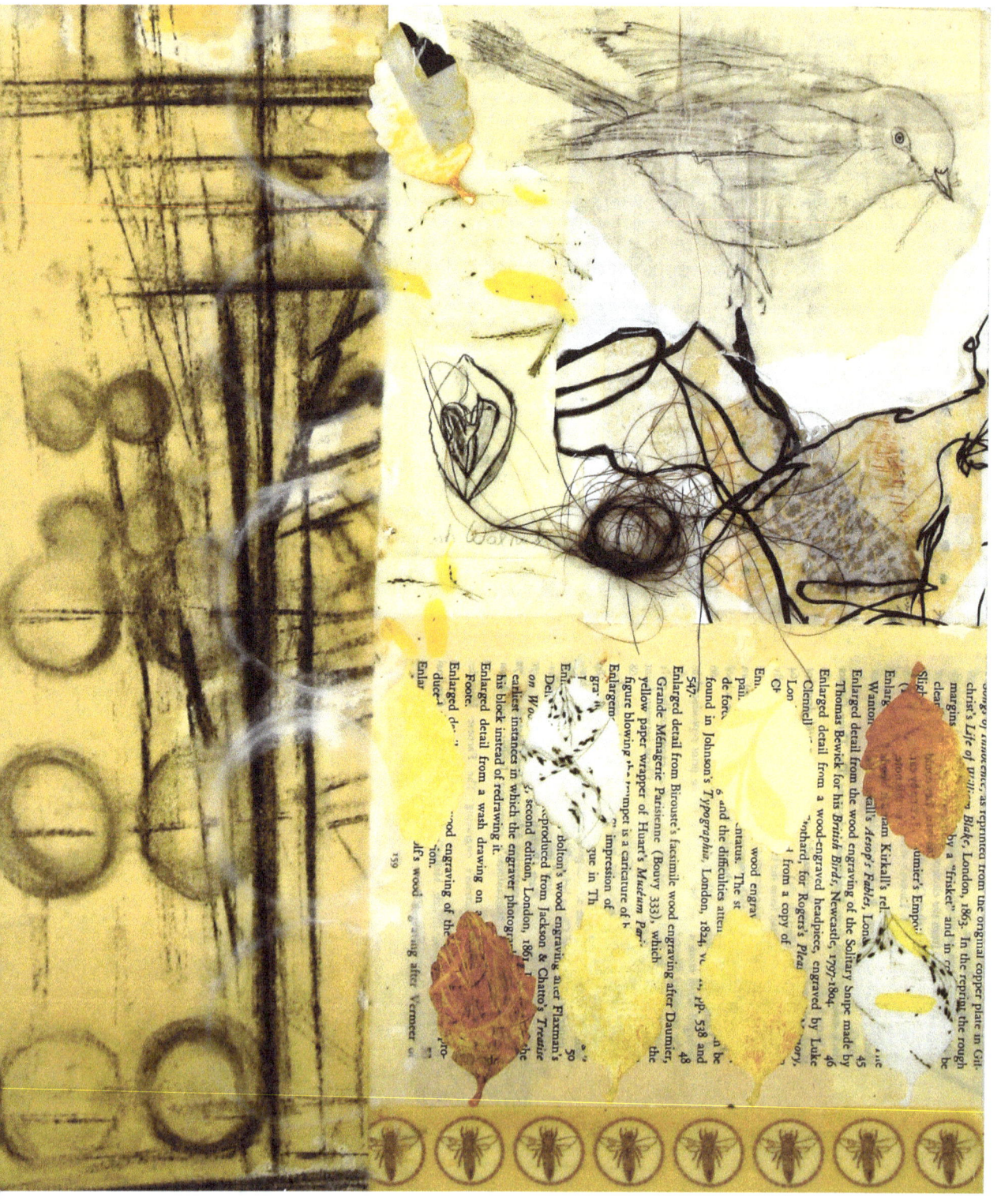

"She Prefers the English Walnut Tree"
Owned by Diane Patton

CONTENTS

Introduction 7

FIRST LAYERS 9
FINDING NEW LAYERS 27
LAYERS OF INSPIRATION 43
WORKING IN LAYERS 59
MAKING ENCAUSTIC COLLAGE 73
LAYERS OF DESIGN 91
DETAILS IN THE LAYERS 107
EXTRA LAYERS 137
LATER LAYERS 151

An Ekphrastic Poem 164
Conclusion 166
Resources 170
Sharon Mirtaheri 171

6

INTRODUCTION

This is a story of coming to know myself; the journey that brought me and my love of salvaging to art and how it led to a passion for encaustic wax collage—an ancient and versatile medium. This path showed me that what I had thought of myself for so many years—due to my childhood—was wrong.

First Layers

A lifelong interest in creating things began when I was a child. Yet, as a child, I had no one to nurture that interest. At age sixteen, I began a thirty-year career as a hairstylist which both fulfilled my desire to be creative and provided a living. I took this work further than any stylist I have personally known, doing photo shoots for an international hair fashion magazine and competing in hair styling competitions.

At forty-six, I "gifted" myself an education in studio art, receiving a Bachelor of Arts degree in 2010 (Magna cum Laude with honors in printmaking) and a Masters of Arts in Liberal Studies in 2013 with a concentration in Encaustic Wax Collage.

It is never too late to have a happy childhood.

—Tom Robbins

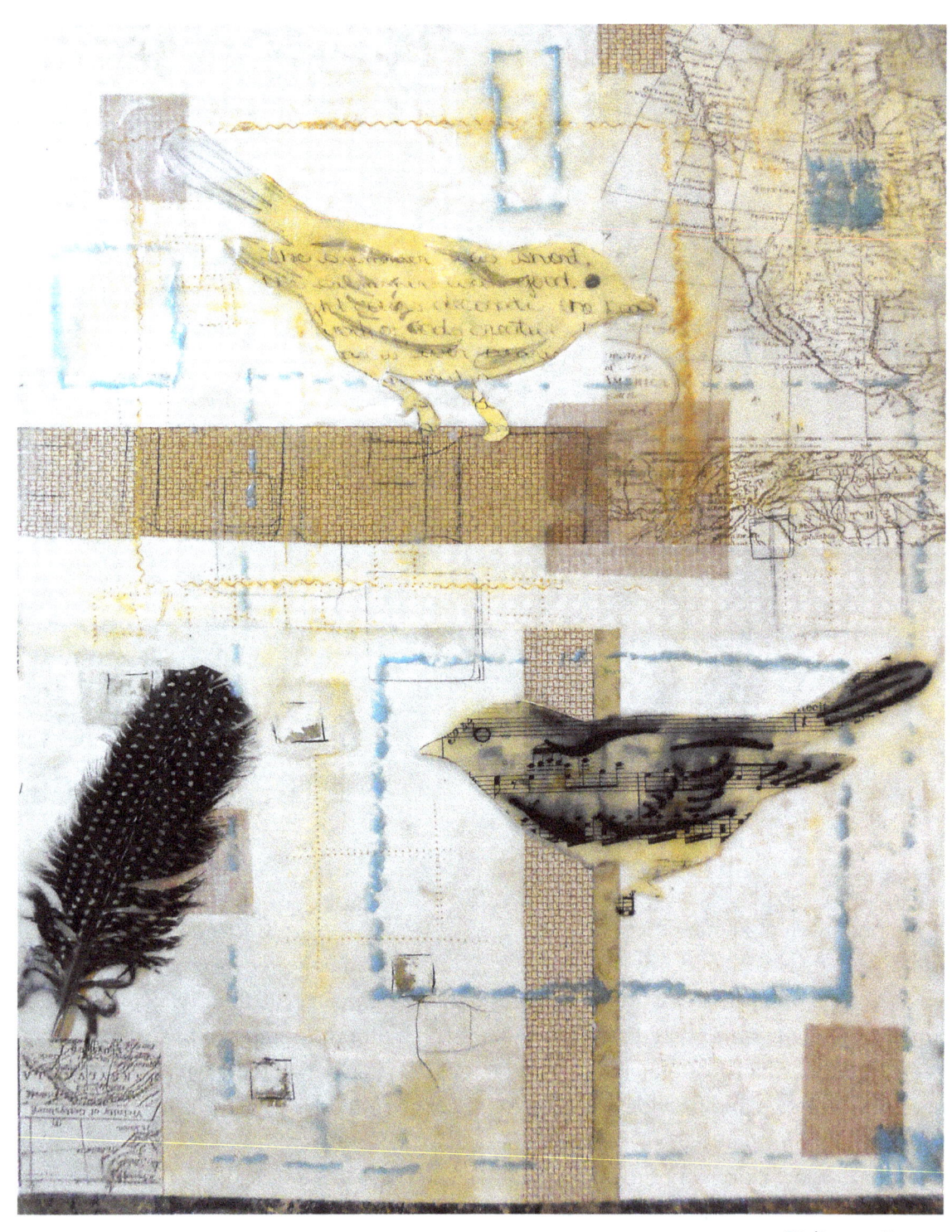

Giulietta e Romeo
Encaustic wax collage on wood panel, 12" × 17" (30cm × 43cm)

I grew up in Radford, Virginia as the eldest daughter of a family whose heritage has remained in the Appalachian Mountains for over a hundred and fifty years. My mother's parents were dairy farmers and Appalachian themes such as quilting, weaving of memory, storytelling, farming, gardening and mountain landscapes began surfacing in my creative expression and continue to inform my artwork.

As a child, my interest in creative outlets was always there, but there was no one in my life who could give me direction. Additionally, the rural school I attended did not deem art important enough to include in its curriculum.

I have a memory of being at our family's picnic table outdoors, in the heat of the summer, with drawing paper and a pencil set—a Christmas present I had asked for and was excited to have received. It included an instruction book on how to draw using the grid method. I was in fifth or sixth grade. After many hours of trying diligently, I did not achieve any results that looked like my expectations, and so I gave up. I don't think anyone around me at that time even noticed.

My very favorite things to play with as a child were items I would drag out of the trash. Pill bottles became needed items for role-playing as a pharmacist. I would sneak junk mail out of the trash can and play mailwoman; delivering it to all the underwear drawers in the house. (Poor mother!)

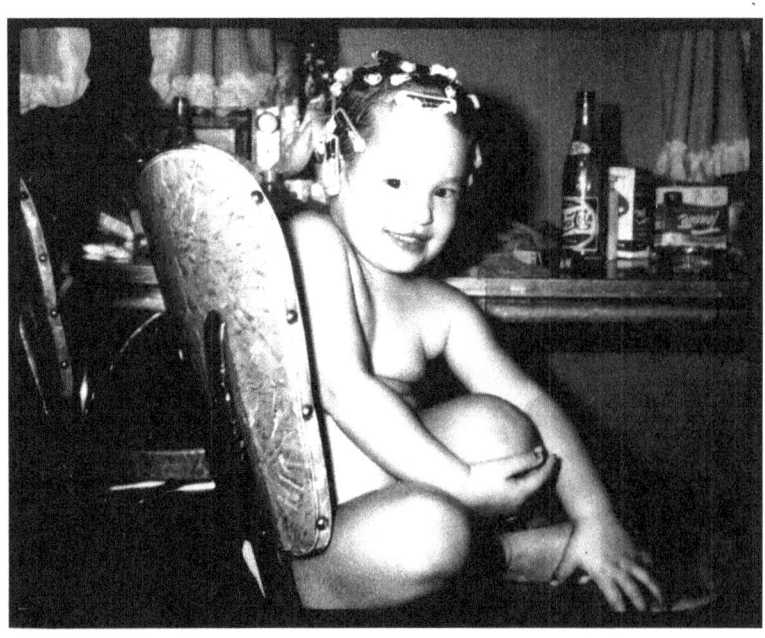

My love of plants began at an early age, and a very happy place for me as a child was in the garden at Grannie's farm.

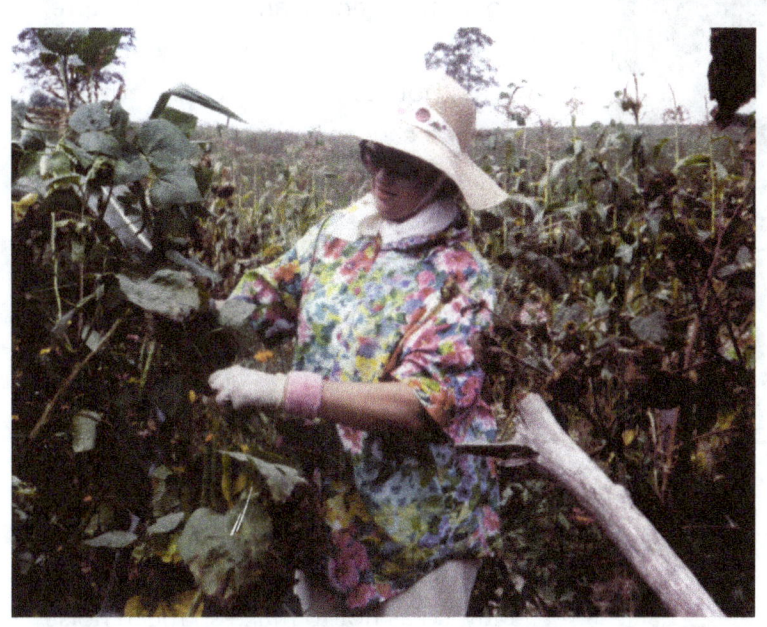

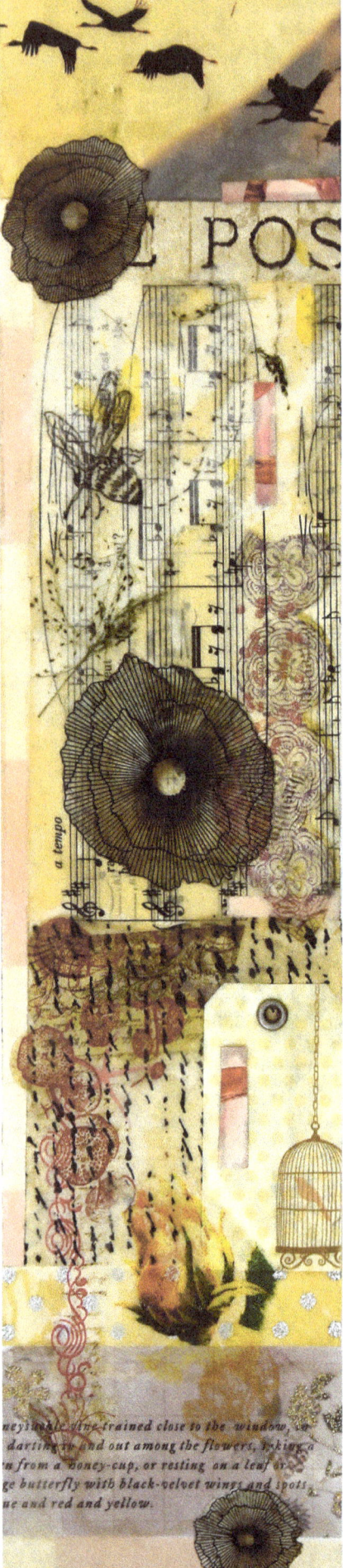

Every Saturday, Aunnie (my mother's sister) came to get us and took us grocery shopping downtown, as Ma did not drive. Occasionally in the heat of the summers, Ma and Aunnie would go window shopping at the Grand Piano Furniture store. The store would give you free baby Cokes in glass bottles that tasted far better than Coke in a can, and I would stay with the pianos in the window while they looked at furniture deeper in the store.

  I would walk around the back peering in at the inner workings of the piano, running my hands over the slick, smooth, glossy black wood, and eventually make my way to the bench. I would just sit there looking at the gleaming keys until I could bear it no more. I had to touch and hear the sound the keys made. I did it ever so gently, so as not to make so much noise that the sales lady would come tell me to stop. I asked for a piano every Christmas

Life Free, Life Caged
Encaustic wax collage on wood panel, 3½" × 15½"
(9cm × 32cm)

from the time I was six until I was thirteen when I finally understood there was no money for a piano.

    Knowing there would never be money for a piano, I took clarinet lessons for four or five years in grade and high school because the instrument could be rented. I had braces on my teeth and was told what to play, not asked. It did not speak to me the way the gleaming piano did.

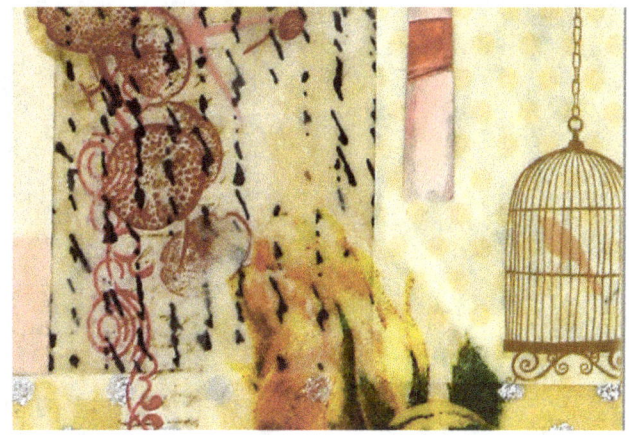

There were other things I asked for every Christmas and never received such as a Spirograph drawing tool, which I had seen advertised on television. I wanted Legos like the boys across the street had and was told they were for boys, not girls.

   I was always a creative child and although we were fairly poor, I did have *some* toys. I had a Barbie Doll when I was three; having been born the same year Barbie hit the market. When I was six, my younger sister and I shared plastic pretend dishes and a pink cardboard stove and sink that actually squirted water. We spent many hours on the porch in the summers playing house as well as playing with paper dolls, which I enjoyed.

Yellow Breasted Bird
Encaustic wax collage on wood panel
5" × 8" (13cm × 20cm)

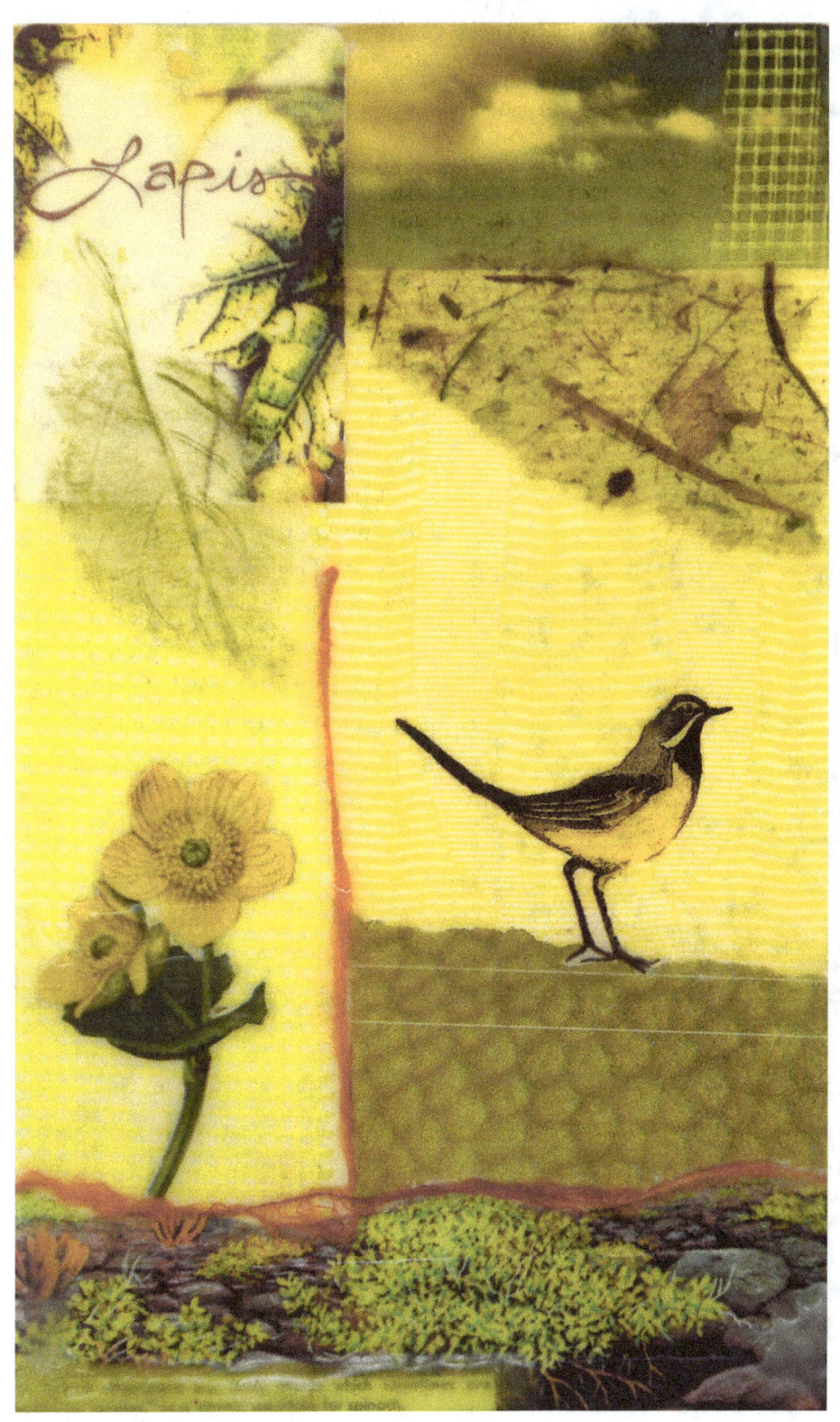

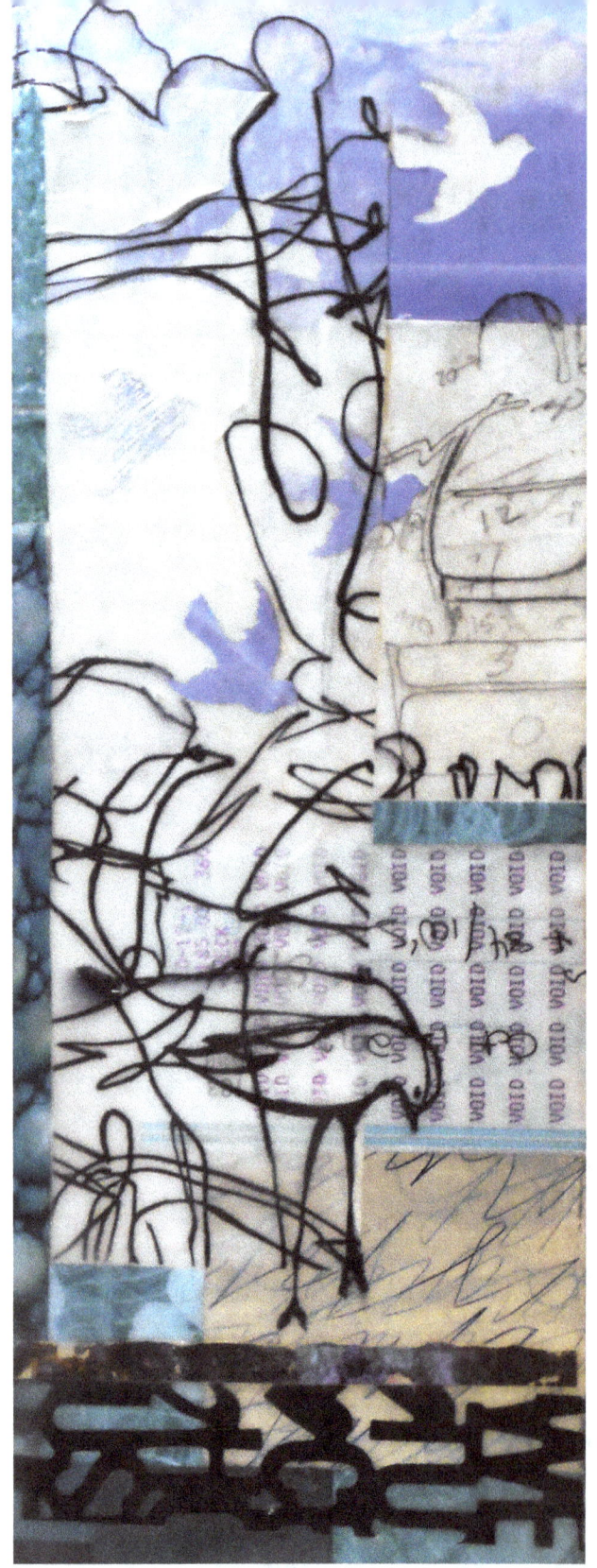

By far, I preferred crayons and coloring books to my toys. Ma could not buy them for me fast enough. By twelve, that morphed into wonderful oil paint-by-number sets. When I got married at sixteen, I finished the Lord's Supper in paint by numbers. It took me two years to complete and the painting was given to an old boyfriend's mother as a gift.

Flight Pattern
Encaustic wax collage on wood panel
4" × 10" (10cm × 25cm)

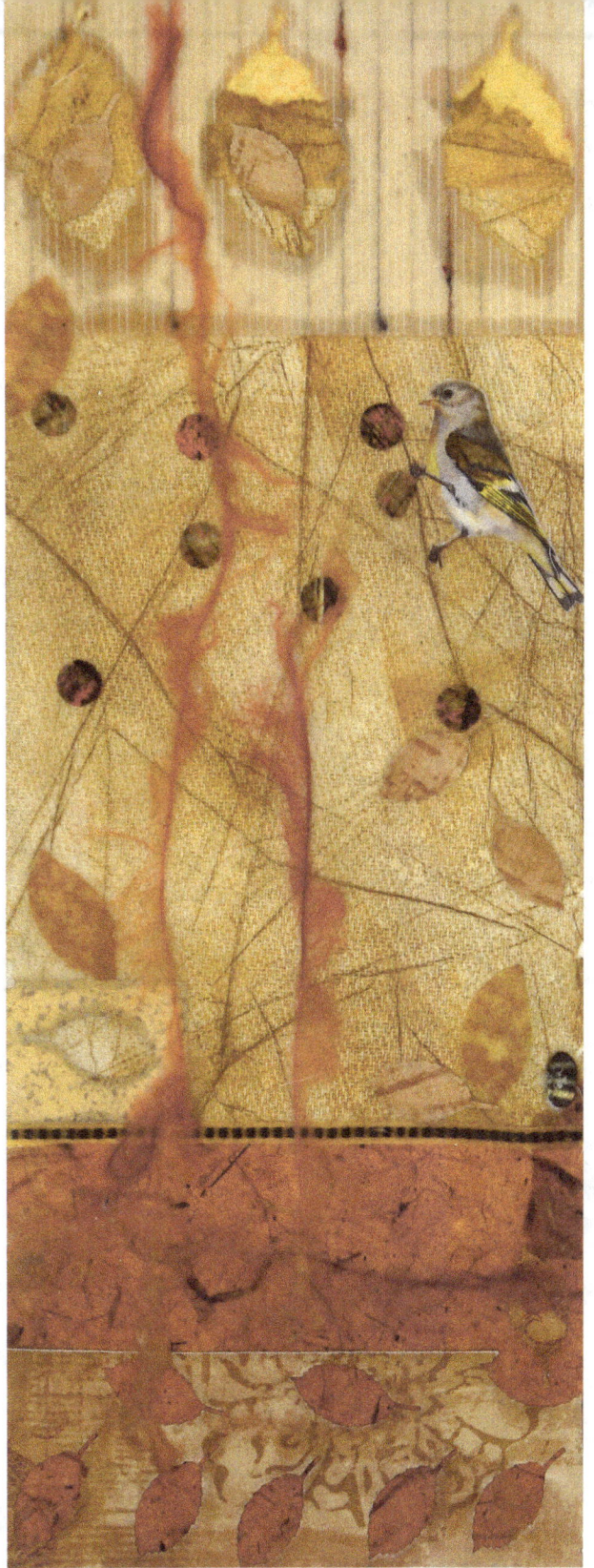

Knowing my family did not have the financial resources to send me to college—as well as having been told by my father on numerous occasions, "You ain't eva gonna 'mount to nuthin"—I unfortunately believed I was stupid and not smart enough to go to college. Being forced in first grade to switch from being left-handed to right-handed and having an undiagnosed learning disability did not help my efforts.

Ripe for the Plucking
Encaustic wax collage on wood panel
5" × 13¾" (10cm × 50cm)

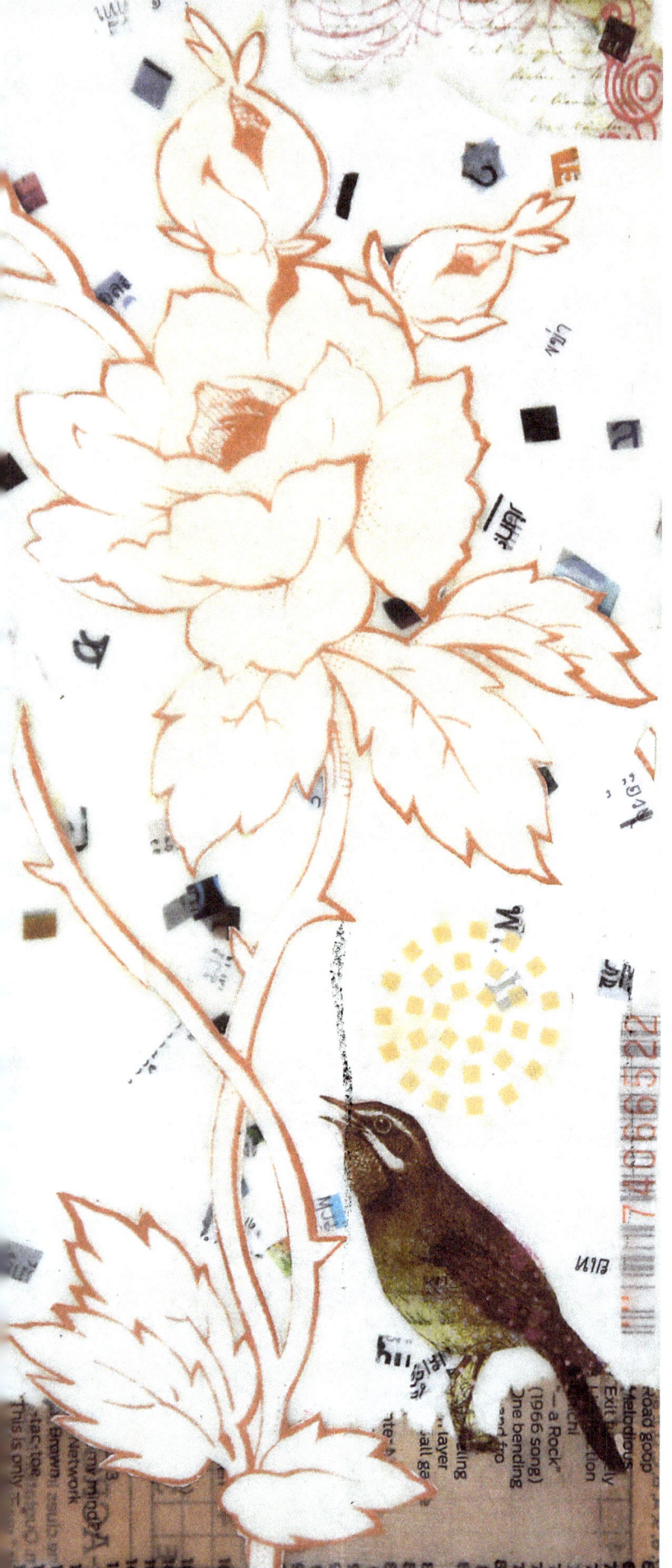

In high school I took cosmetology at Christiansburg Vocational Tech in south-west Virginia and began my first job in a hair salon the day after graduation. I worked for five years in Blacksburg, Virginia and for twenty five years in Gaithersburg, Maryland.

I loved my career as a stylist! But I always felt that I had missed out on something important. Having a highly-educated clientele in the D.C. area made me sure of it.

Song of Gratitude
Encaustic wax collage on wood panel
4" × 9" (10cm × 23cm)

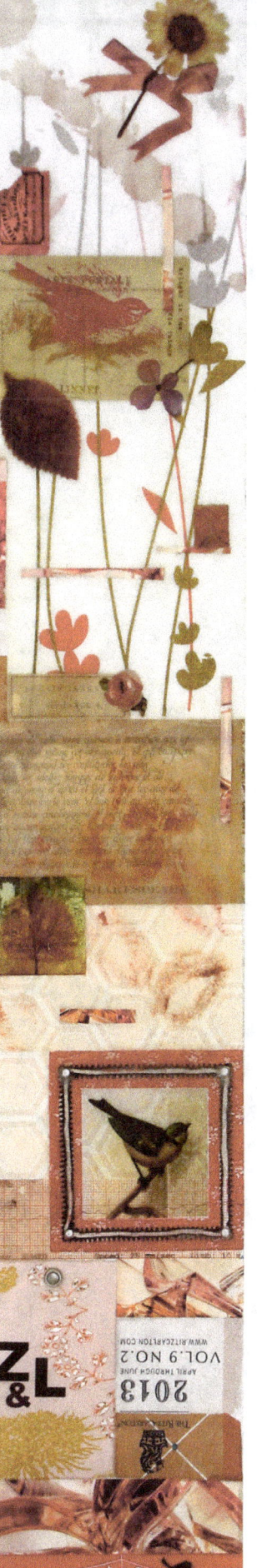

Denny Arrant—a master painter—was a client of a salon I worked at in Maryland and we became close friends. With a longing to explore painting beyond paint-by-numbers, I took private oil painting lessons with Denny, which put me on an adult path of nourishing my creativity.

After completing lessons with Denny, I later began oil-painting lessons with Betsy Koepenick, another successful regional artist. Not long after that, I was asked to be a guest artist on a studio art tour event and I sold half of my paintings, which gave me the confidence to consider a degree in studio art.

La Vie en Rose (The World in Pink)
Encaustic wax collage on wood panel
4" × 24½" (10cm × 62cm)

After thirty years as a hairstylist—and several moves around Virginia and Maryland—I wanted to come home. I needed rotator-cuff surgery and was no longer able to work full-time again, so I retired. My husband and I moved to Salem, Virginia in early 2004. It was time to make dreams come true.

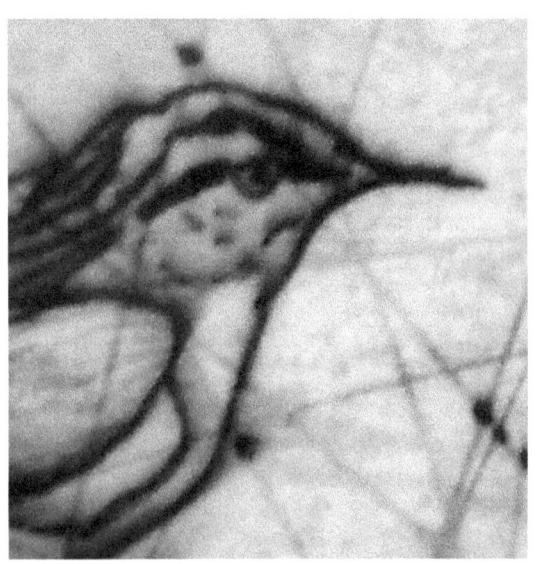

How to Escape
Encaustic wax collage on wood panel
5" × 9" (13cm × 23cm)

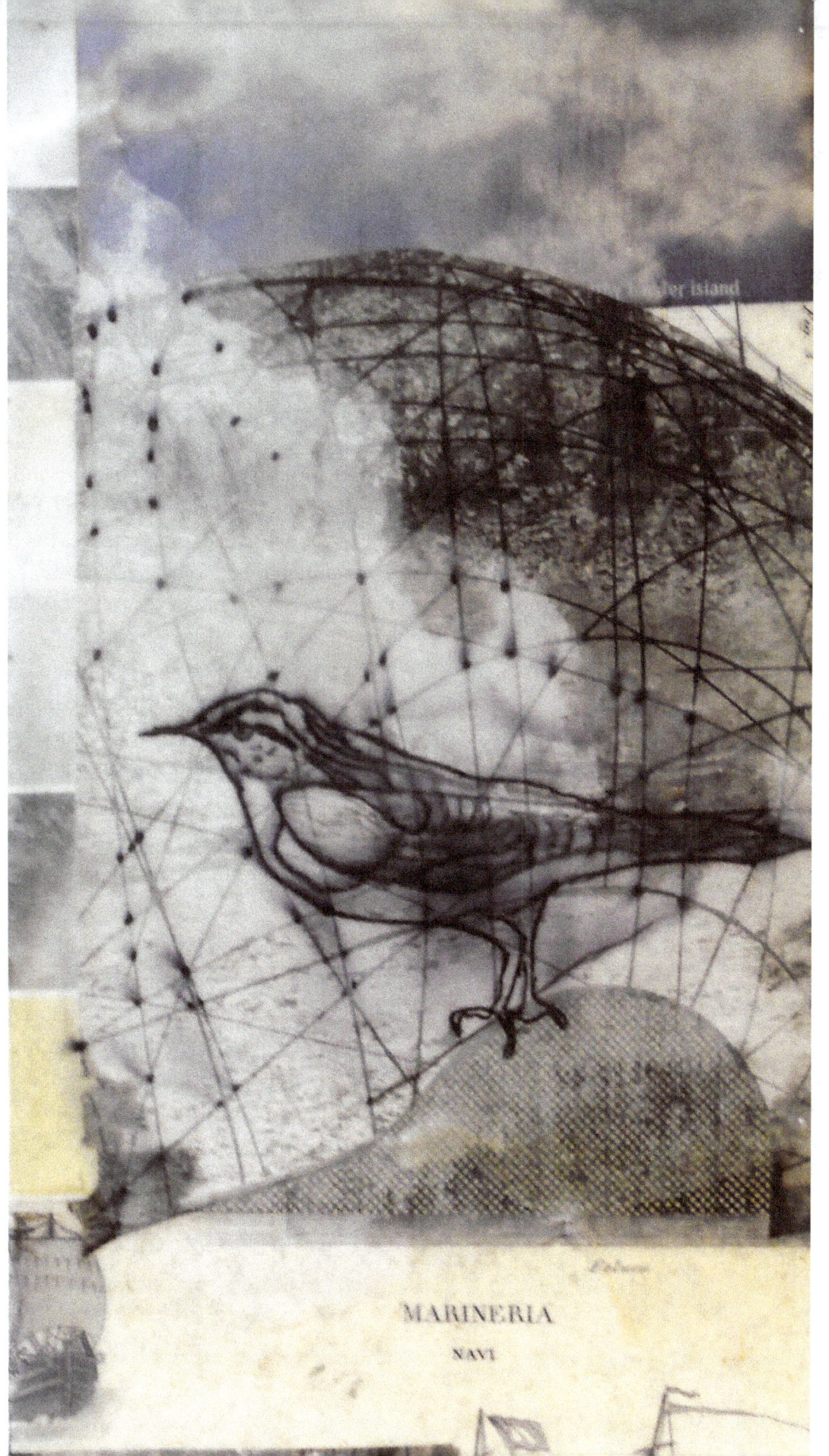

Entering into retirement, my husband and I moved to Roanoke, Virginia. In my first year in Roanoke, while waiting to get the in-state tuition rate, I founded "Angels with Scissors," a charity organization for the Roanoke Rescue Mission with forty-five salons and one hundred and fifty stylists joining me in raising funds to build a three-chair hair salon inside the Mission's Battered-Women's Shelter building.

There is now a place for stylists to volunteer to cut hair for the homeless, battered women and children, and men and women enrolled in the recovery program.

There was no place to go in Radford back then when my mother, sister and I really needed a safe haven, so doing this work at this shelter meant the world to me and I am grateful to this day to everyone who supported—and continues to support—this worthy cause.

Inspired
Encaustic wax collage on wood panel
7½" × 15½" (19cm × 39cm)

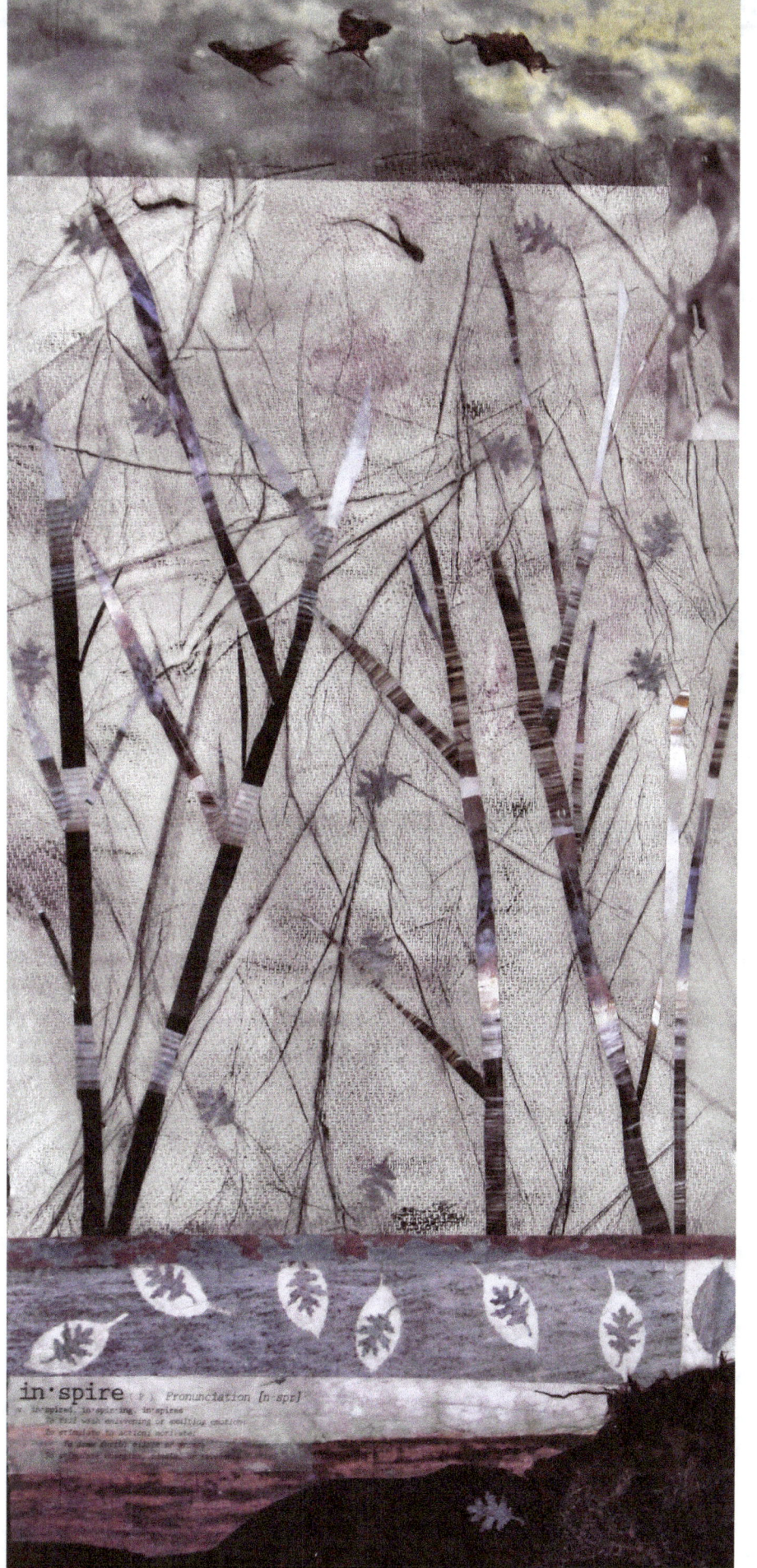

Finding New Layers

When a new exploration really speaks to you—as encaustic wax did to me—you find a way to make it serve you. Life is like that also. If you want something badly enough, you can make it happen. You need to believe in yourself; no one else can do that for you.

With my hair-stylist career having come to a close, I yearned to prove to myself that I could have a college education.

During the autumn of my forty-sixth year, when I opened the letter of acceptance from Hollins University, I fell into my husband's arms sobbing. I was equally overjoyed and terrified. I began a full-time educational journey at Hollins University in 2005 when I started work on a Liberal Arts degree. Even though my goal was a broad education in Liberal Arts, I also owed it to myself to pursue a major in studio art and a minor in creative writing. When I finished my undergraduate degree in 2010 I was not ready to leave and continued with classes for a Masters of Liberal Arts (MALS) degree. I was the first student at Hollins to finish my last two undergrad classes while also taking my first two MALS classes. At the time, the policy was to be admitted only with undergrad degree in hand, which I thought ridiculous. The president of the college at the time, President Nancy Gray, however, went to bat for me so I could start work on the advanced degree.

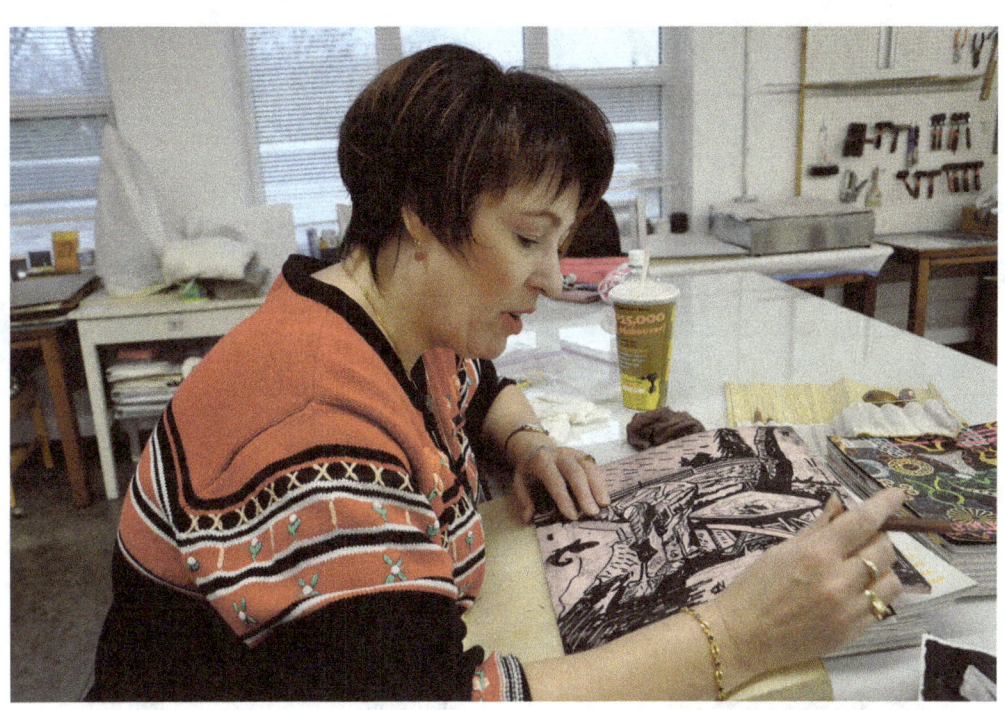

Photo of me taken by Professor Nancy Dahlstrom, Hollins University Print Lab.

My last art class for my MALS degree was an independent study in encaustic wax collage with Professor Nancy Dahlstrom. I relied on her for art critiques. I, however, taught myself encaustics as it was not being taught at Hollins while I was there.

It was a good lesson for me to experience self-directed education as it would serve me for the rest of my life as an artist.

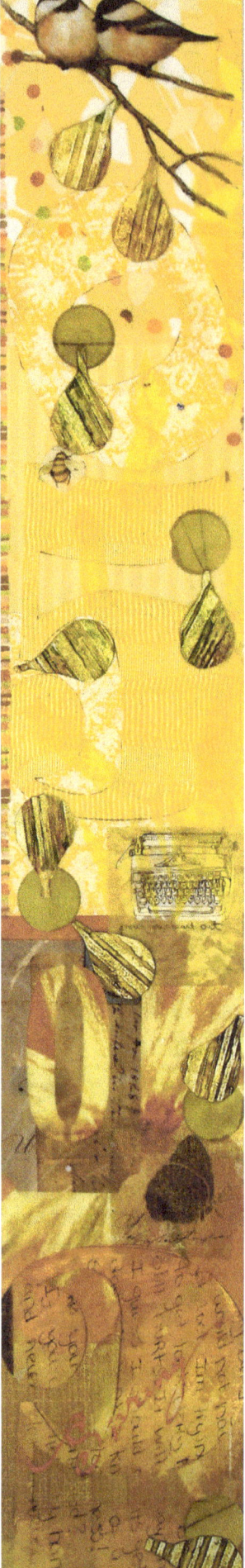

Professor Dahlstrom was most generous with me that last semester of my undergraduate study in giving me a large walled off space in the print lab that became, as one student exclaimed, "a real studio!"

   I dragged all my supplies from home, including etching and monotype materials, and things I had collected for collage over the years. It took three days to set up the space. It was worth it because it inspired me to go at it full tilt. Like other professional artists, I had photos of artist's works on the walls of my studio space as inspiration. I looked upon it as one would look at a job with regular eight-hour days, five days a week.

The Things That Healed Me
Encaustic wax collage on wood panel
4" × 24½" (10cm × 62cm)

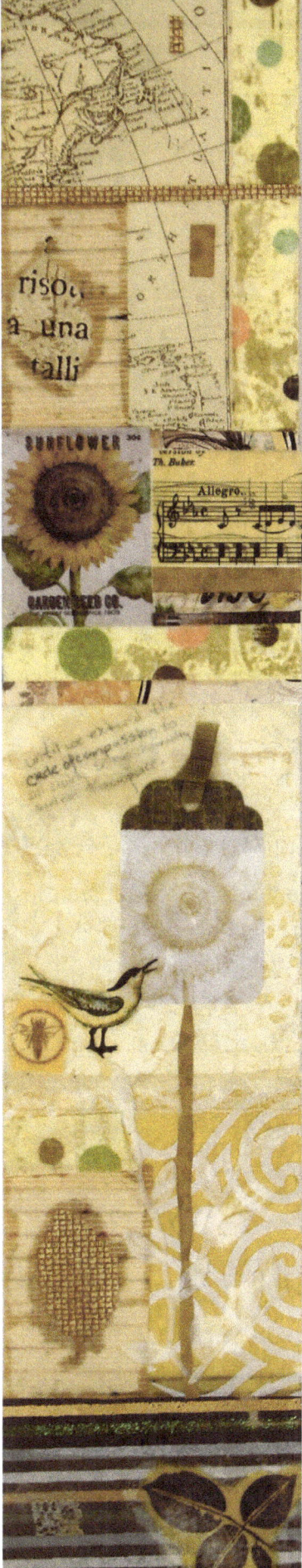

The body of work I achieved was cohesive and large and at the end of the semester Professor Dahlstrom wanted me to have a showing of my work with an opening, just like one would in a gallery. Although the show was not planned until the end of the semester and unusual for a MALS student as this body of work was a class and not thesis work, I learned exactly what it takes to promote myself and be successful as an artist by organizing a show.

The opening was well attended and of thirty-eight pieces, twenty-seven sold before or during the opening. The rest sold shortly after, and several were in juried art shows winning first place, second place, and an honorable mention.

Sing Allegro
Encaustic wax collage on wood panel
4" × 20½" (10cm × 52cm)

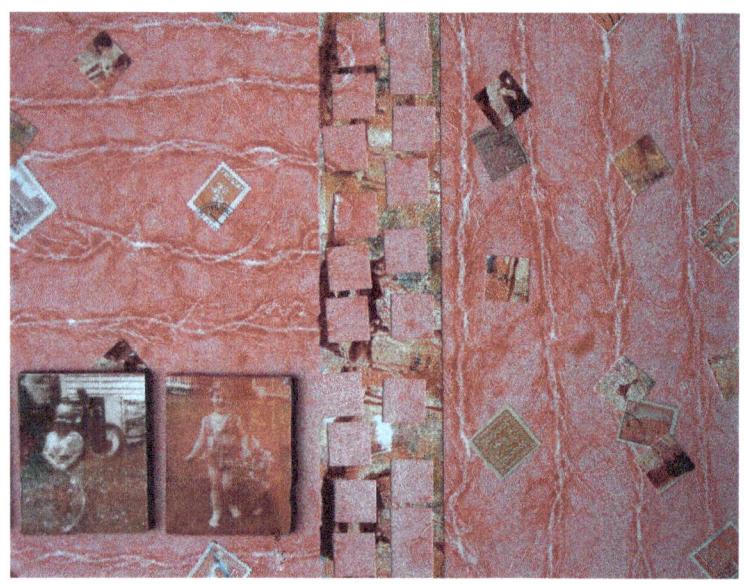

Fuzzy Memories
Printmaking paper and muslin
19" × 17" (48cm × 43cm)
Solar plate etchings, stamps, hand colored papers on monotype

Creating solar plates is a way to get an etched plate that is permanent using scanned photos, ink jet printer on Mylar, and the sun, or a photo lab light exposure.

While experimenting with these plates, I loved using assorted punches and incorporating the punched pieces combined with leftover negative paper into my work.

While integrating solar plate etchings into my monotype pieces, I deliberately chose photos of my childhood that depicted happy moments, which is not generally how I view or remember my childhood. In writing my memoir, I have been dealing with issues of memory: what is truth in memory; fuzzy, faded memory and gaps in memory? These interests have translated into this body of monotype work. (See page 122 for another example of this use.)

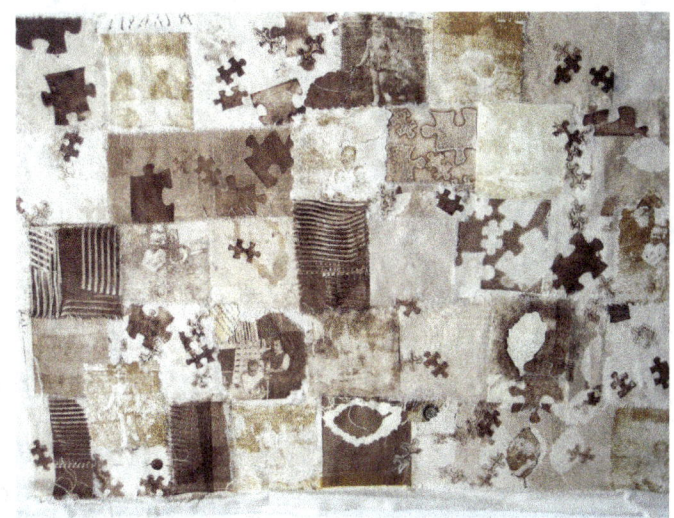

These are many 3" × 3" (8cm ×8cm) squares glued down to fabric like a quilt. There are sixteen solar plate images in varying degrees of clarity. Some are barely visible while others are very clear, mimicking memory. I ripped the muslin leaving raw edges.

Pieced Memory
Mono print on muslin fabric
26" × 17" (66cm × 43cm)

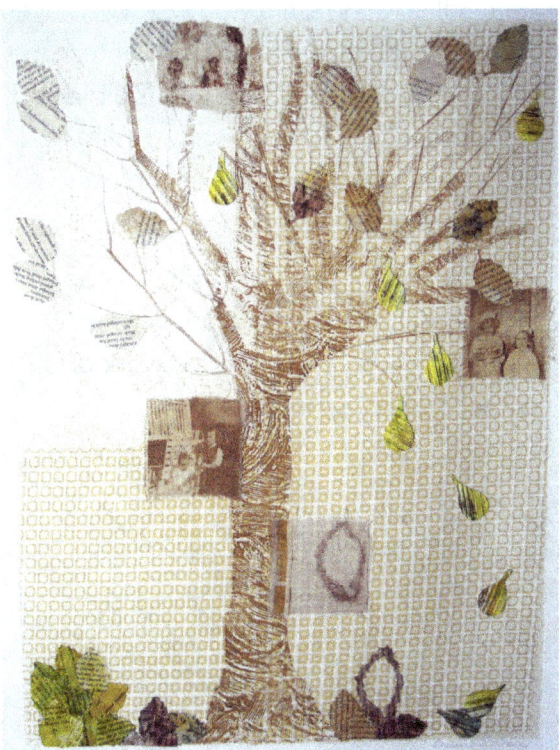

This piece is a metaphor for my family. Some of the fruit was rotten from alcohol and alcoholism. The tree stencil was cut from a textured wallpaper. The branches were made using dried organic matter and inked in raw umber. The background was a ghost print from another piece in which I used a square hook rug fabric as a resist. The leaves on the left are from punched paper from an old art book. The leaves on the right are the same method but are hand tinted. The pears are cut out from textured wallpaper and tinted green and yellow.

Fruit Hangs Heavy on Some Sides
Printmaking paper
20" × 28" (51cm × 71cm)

My father was an alcoholic. His choice of drink during the week was Pabst beer and then hard alcohol on the weekends. I hated the smell of it and when I bought two cases and poured it down the drain for this piece, I gagged the entire time. The sharp edges of the cut tin reference the danger my mother, sister and I lived in constantly. We walked on egg shells around him never knowing when his rage would explode—drunk or not.

I got married the day after my sixteenth birthday to escape the abuse. My mother, however, did not escape, as there was no Rescue Mission or Battered Women's Shelter in Radford in the 60s or 70s. She died at forty-eight from a heart condition that was exacerbated by the abuse she endured for decades. I was twenty-four.

Through prayer and through the healing act of being creative, I have come to understand that although the childhood I had was sad, it has given me an abundance of compassion for other hurting souls.

Pieces of a poem are tucked into the dress and around the edges of the dress. I always viewed my mother as an angel and I have portrayed her as such based on a famous painting at The National Portrait Gallery in Washington D.C. by Thayer. Her dress looks similar to the painted one in Thayer's angel and the belt is a piece of my mother's costume jewelry. I imagined what holds feathers in place and used a beeswax candle for the scaffolding.

I took the collage class at Hollins after having a recurring dream in which I saw this piece of artwork. My work often comes from dreams.

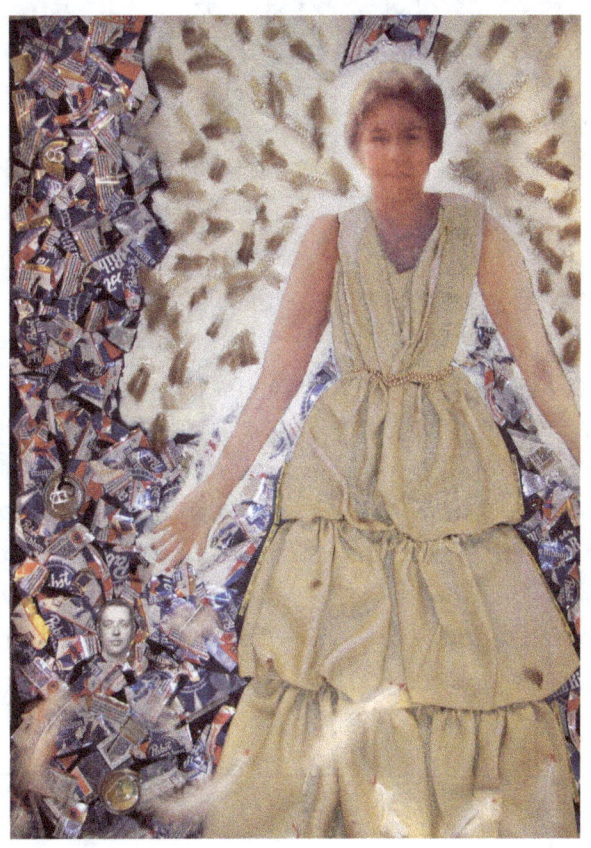

Flailing the Angel
Mixed media: tin, burlap, feathers, bees wax comb, costume jewelry, oil paint, paper on Masonite.
30" × 48" (76cm × 122cm)

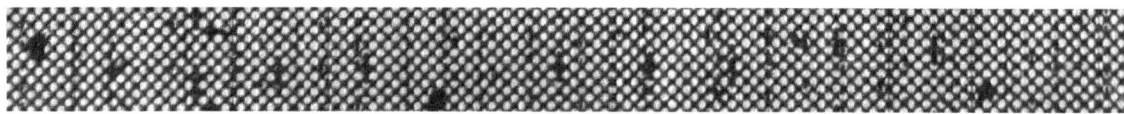

During my senior year at Hollins I began a nice relationship with a very talented local interior designer who gave me discontinued high-end wallpaper books and fabric sample books. My basement is now full of these (much to my spouse's chagrin). I took my portfolio with me when I introduced myself to the interior designer and showed him my work and how I use discarded items. I asked if he would give me these items rather than tossing them in the dumpster. He was thrilled to be recycling and even told me that if I worked on a larger scale he would throw some business my way. I took that as the compliment.

At the end of every semester while I was at Hollins University, I would go through all the very large trashcans in the art building to retrieve treasure the younger girls would throw out. What a sight it was; older woman with head in can and very large derriere sticking straight up in the air! I found never-used, expensive copper plates from etching class, sketches, not-up-to-snuff monotypes, scraps of canvas, Mylar, and tracing paper. At the end of senior year there were paint brushes, pens, pencils of all kinds, and paints! A lot of items all dumped and unwanted came home with me.

R is for Red, R is for Raven
Encaustic wax collage on wood panel
5" × 8" (13cm × 20cm)

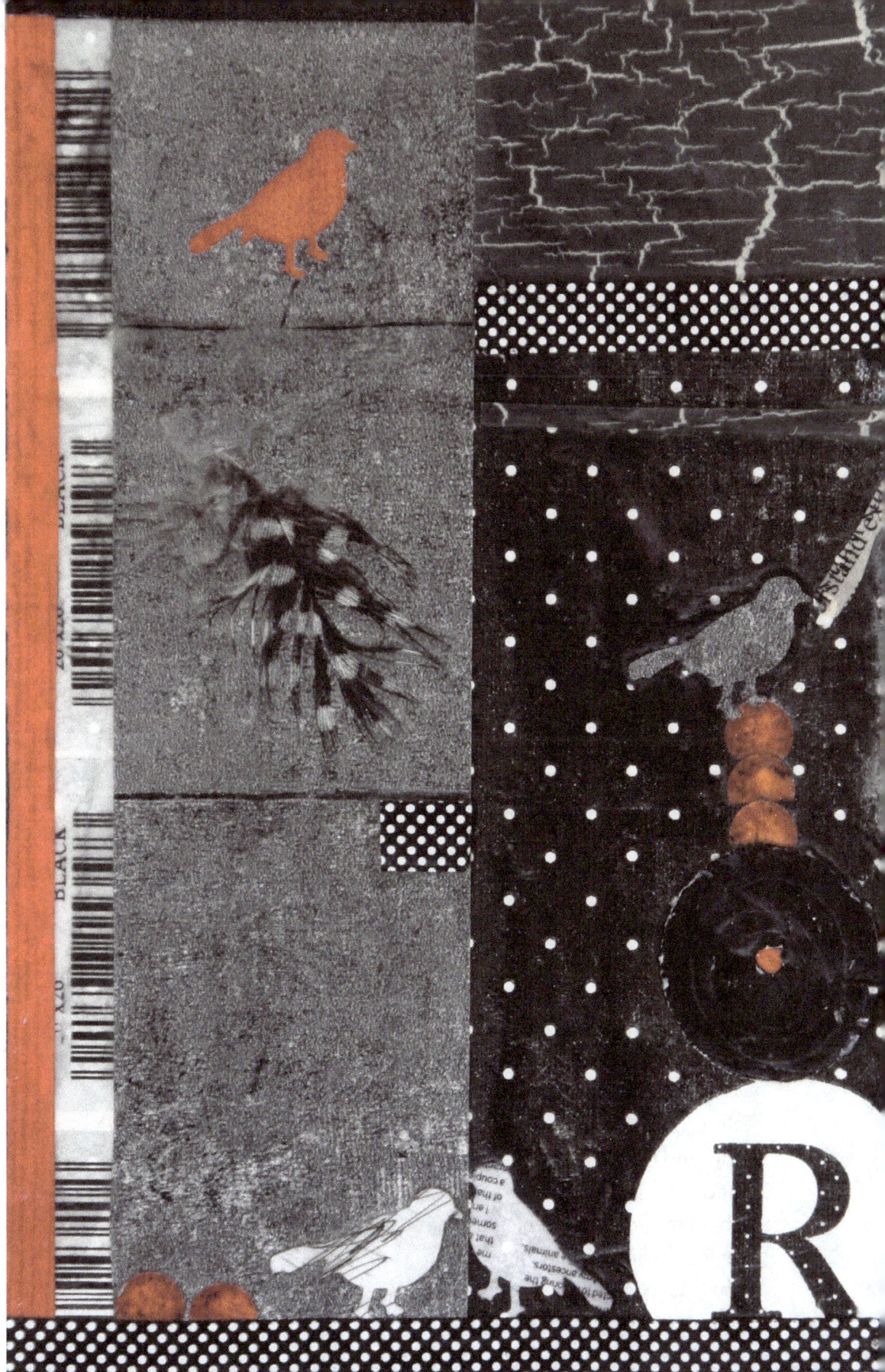

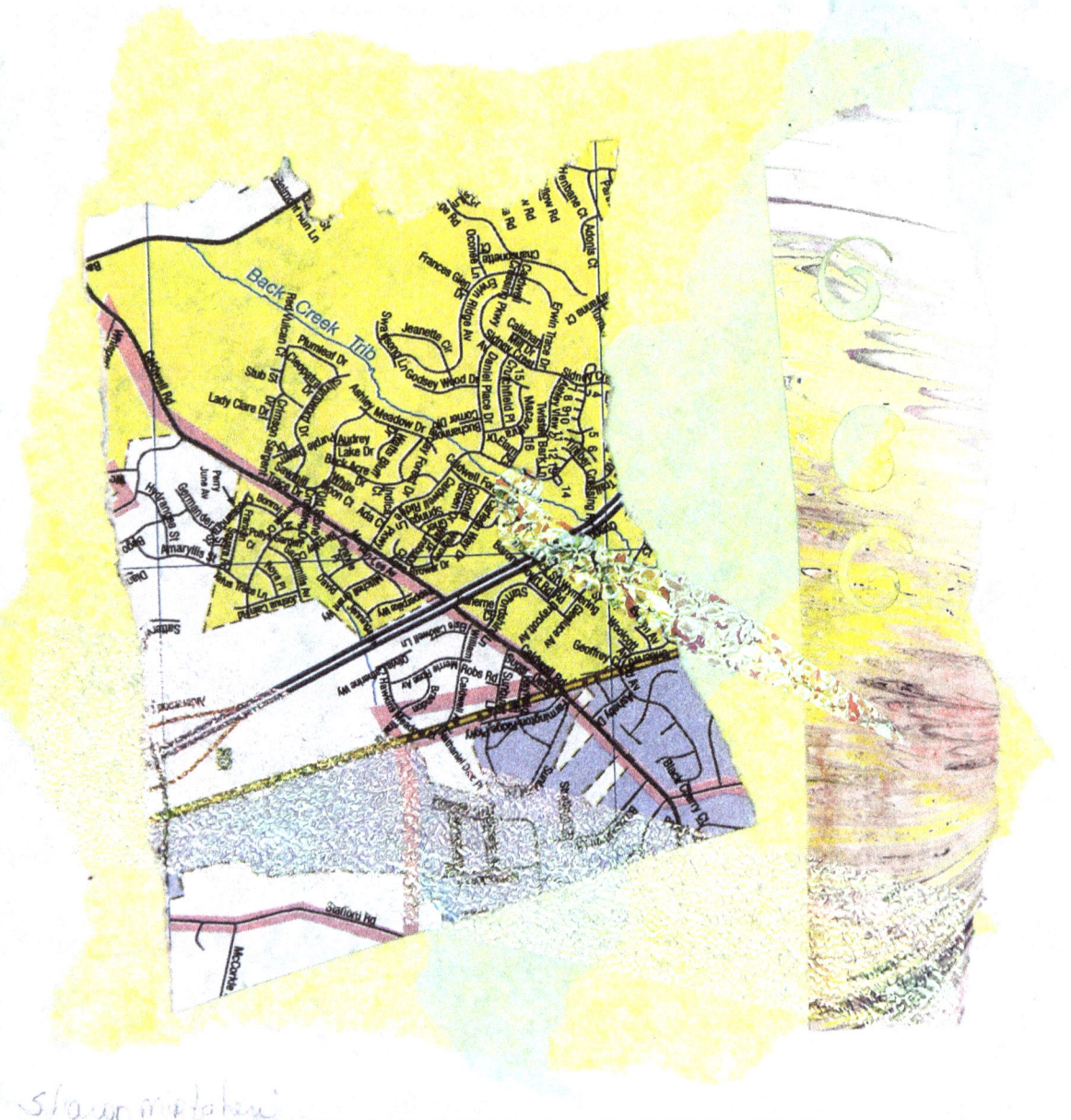

In monotype class, I always disliked wasting the ink on the glass table at the end of a work day. I began to treat myself to "play time" by adding some ink to the mix and rolling the brayer over it and inking up the scrap mat board that I talked my local picture framer into giving me. I am now using that stash in my collage work.

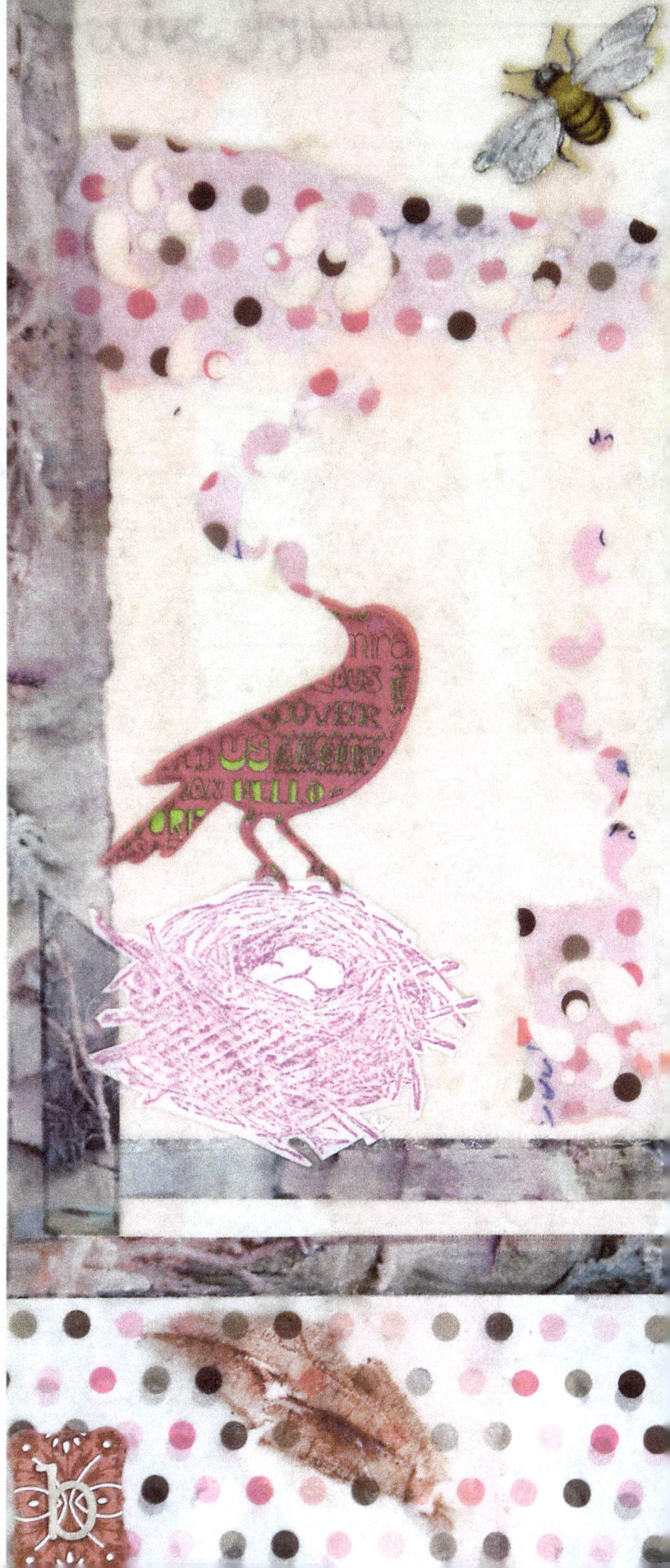

I have survived an extremely violent childhood, the loss of my mother, two divorces and more illnesses than most women my age. I have had to navigate a maze of a road to get to where I stand as an artist, but I am finally here. I had no formal art training either as a child or young adult but "it is never too late to have a happy childhood" so I gifted myself a college education at the age of forty six and I am proud to have completed a Master of Arts in Liberal Studies degree at Hollins University in encaustic wax collage. Not a lot has changed in my personality or my art-making since I was a child. I still look for non-ordinary items to use for creative activity.

Love My Nest
Encaustic wax collage on wood panel
4" × 9" (10cm × 23cm)

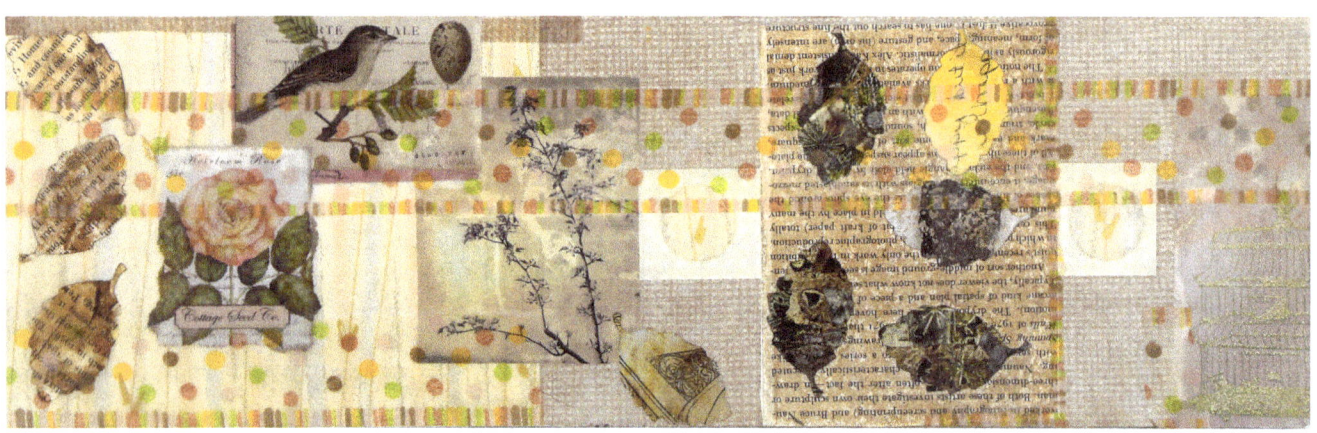

Choices: Happy, Unhappy
Encaustic wax collage on wood panel
17" × 5½" (xxcm × xxcm)

It has been a lifelong dream come true to have a college education. Finally, I am having that happy childhood. There is some irony in the two things I have learned from six years at Hollins that I hold above all others: After making mostly As and graduating Magna Cum Laude, I now see how wrong my father was in his assessment of my intelligence. I am far smarter than he or I ever thought I was.

The other thing I learned is that becoming educated is a lifelong process and never has to end.

Thank you, Hollins, for believing in me and making it possible.

There is inspiration from a quote by Martha Graham that has stuck with me since the day I read it. It speaks to the fact that there is an energy that is special and *unique* to every creator and is passed along to others with every new work created. When we block our creative expression, we miss out on our opportunity to share this unique form of energy with the world.

I feel Martha's words speak to all artists and directs them to listen to that "inside voice" that urges one to be creative and expressive and it gives the reason why.

LAYERS OF INSPIRATION

Art is potent. In order to paint an object one has to really look at it closely—everything around it and the negative space that has nothing in it. To look and really see something is to appreciate it. Art acts like a mirror to society of what is good and what is wrong.

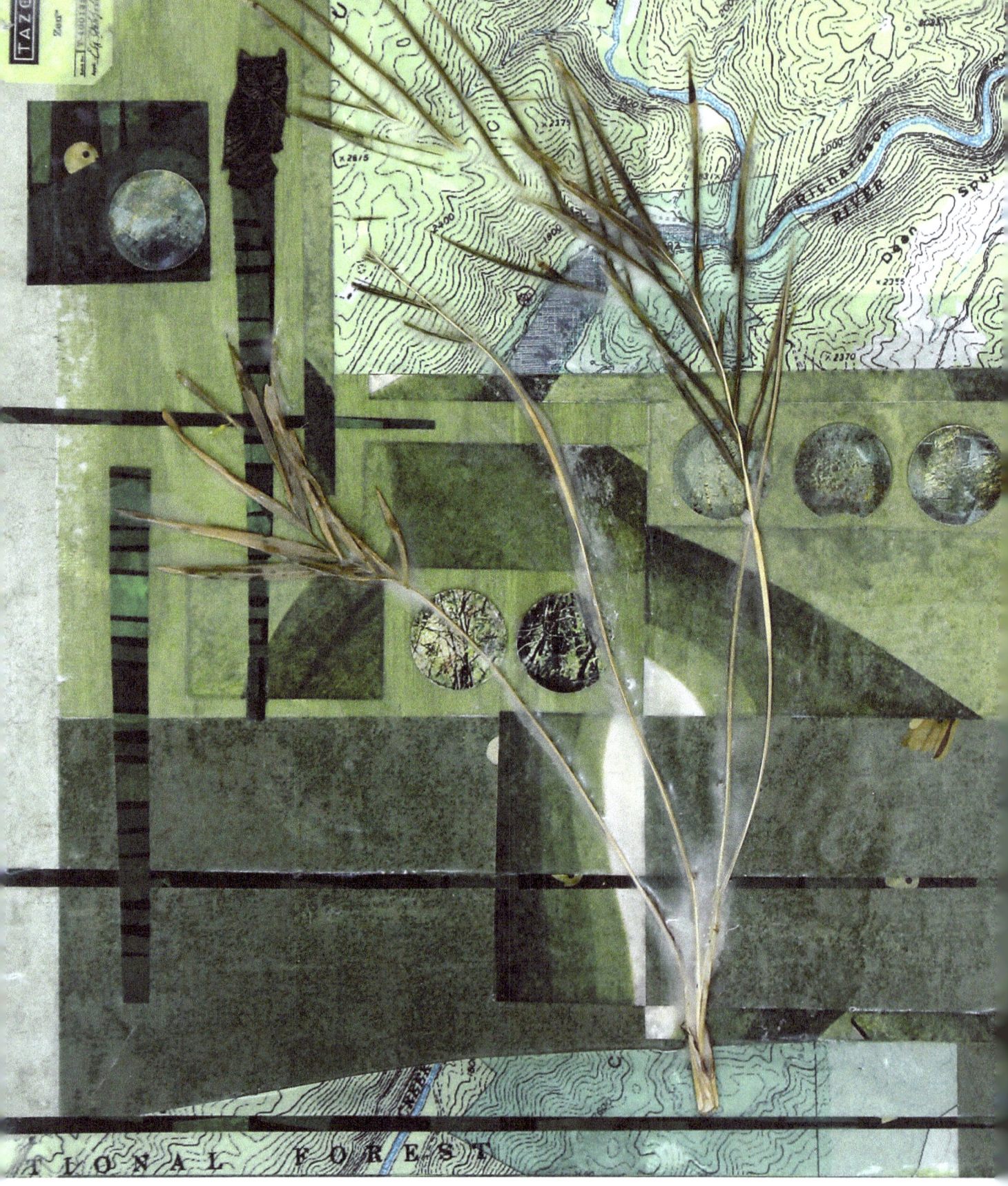

In 2013, when it came time to begin my thesis, I wanted to continue with encaustic wax collage where I left off in that last independent study class. I chose to make it an educational tool on what is possible in encaustics. And while every artist owes a debt to the inspiration from all artists that came before him or her, it was important to me to focus not so much on the inspiration that came to me from other artists, but that which I get daily from the immense creativity of nature itself.

It was my love of gardening that first drew me to want to take those lessons from Denny Arrant prior to my time at Hollins University. The reason I started to paint was to reduce my melancholy during winter seasons when the garden was put to bed. My idea was that even though my beloved flowers were at rest, if I could paint them, I could bring them back to life—at least in my heart.

National Forrest
Encaustic wax collage on wood panel
12" × 12" (30cm × 30cm)

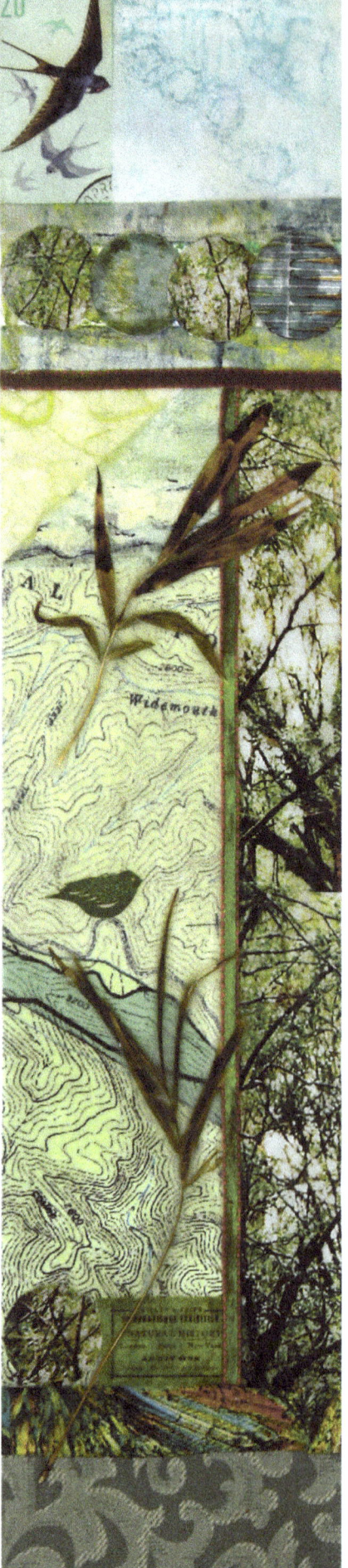

I started my garden from scratch and kept a photo journal from the first day I began gardening to document its progress and took many closeup photos of my flowers. I painted from the photographs and used them as a source for etchings as well. (I still maintain the habit of documenting each piece of artwork both visually and in a written statement about the process I used. I find myself referring to my art journal/diary quite a lot for inspiration.)

Hirundo-Rustica
Encaustic wax collage on wood panel
3½" × 12" (9cm × 30cm)

I feel gardening and paintings are related on so many levels. Gardening and painting are my spiritual practices. I feel painting and creating art is really a prayer asking to be used as an instrument of connection. Many master artists felt this, notably Kandinsky felt this about the use of color being spiritual. He also felt the artist could be a prophet of sorts. I learned about Kandinsky and his color and art theories in an art history class with Professor Kimberly Rhodes at Hollins University.

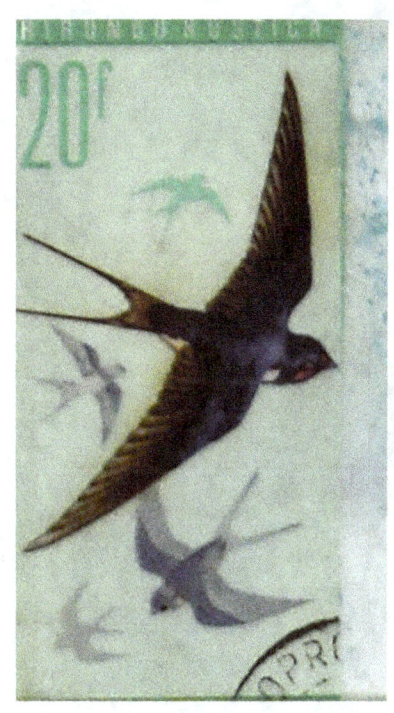

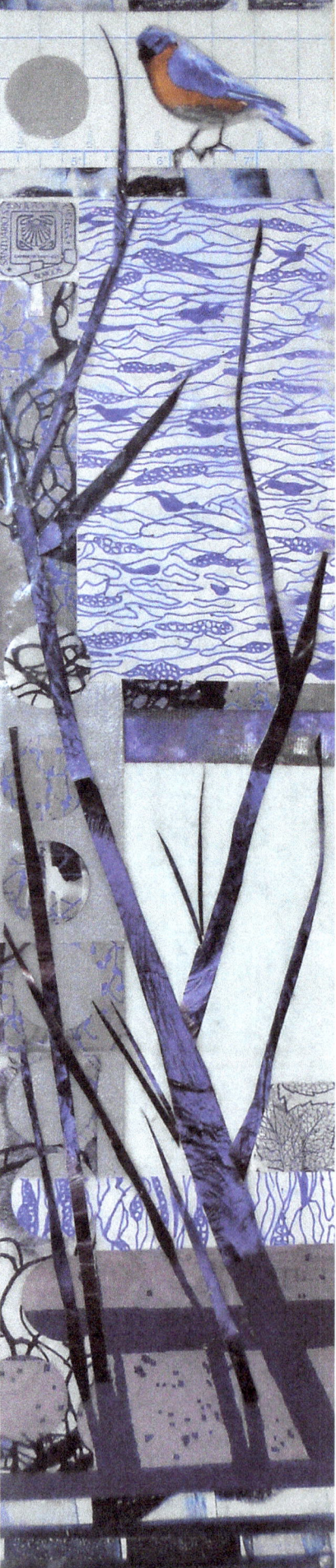

In his book: *The Mission of Art*, modern day visionary artist Alex Gray succeeds in showing the connection of humans to all matter in the universe and to a Higher Power that created all that is known. He believes artists can be the new messengers that enlighten people to this connection. The leaders of religions all over the world go on pilgrimages to his Sacred Mirrors gallery in New York State. Artists have tried to show these connections throughout history and he discusses this at length in his book.

Silver Moon
Encaustic wax collage on wood panel
4" × 19" (10m × 48cm)

Another similarity gardening has to painting is that a gardener really paints the landscape with color, texture, and all the same design principles that an artist uses in creating a work of art. Both are also solitary pursuits that facilitate introspection.

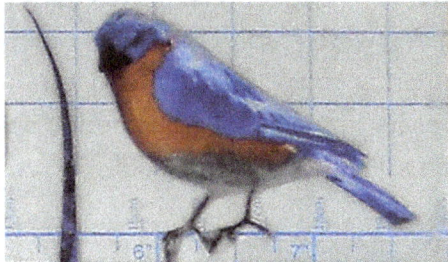

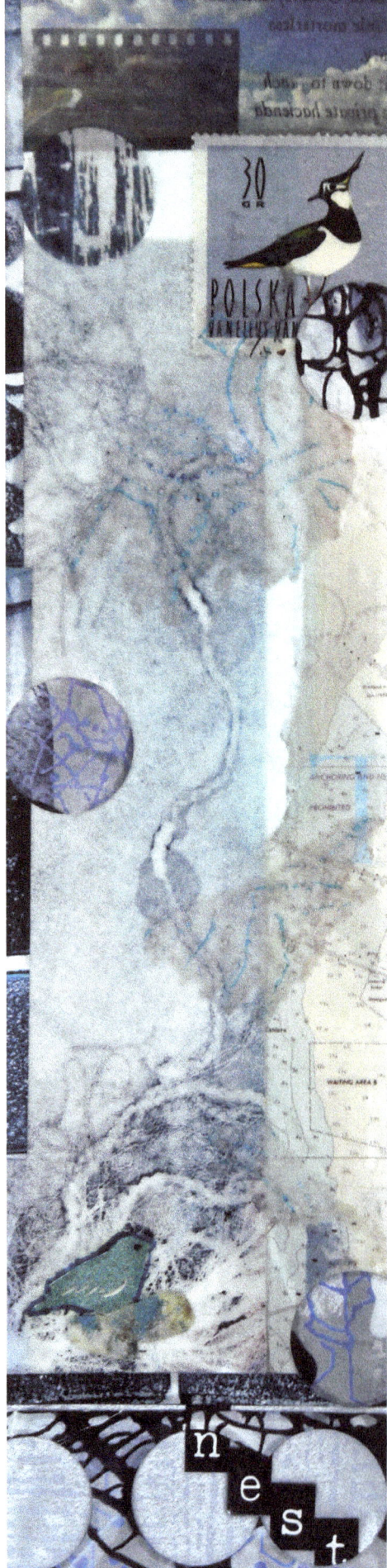

From the time I began exploring this life as an artist, my goal was to try to express the feeling of awe I have in the enormity of variety and beauty of the Divine's creations, as well as the gratitude I feel for these gifts. If my work can make the viewer stop and consider the object I have represented in the same way I stop to view the object in order to appreciate it and represent it, then I have succeeded as an artist.

Nest
Encaustic wax collage on wood panel
3" × 12" (8cm × 30cm)

Time evaporates and falls away and I become lost in the object I am observing. In my mind I cease to exist along with what Buddhists call "the monkey-mind," worries and problems of the past and future. Peace and contentment take over my being. I feel a sense of connectedness to all things divine. These connections are the things that happen to me when I view a landscape, or when I am on my knees in the dirt and stop for a long while to watch a red armored bug crawl across the fuzzy, velveteen stamens of a graceful yellow lily.

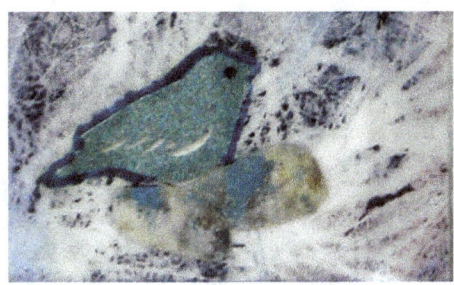

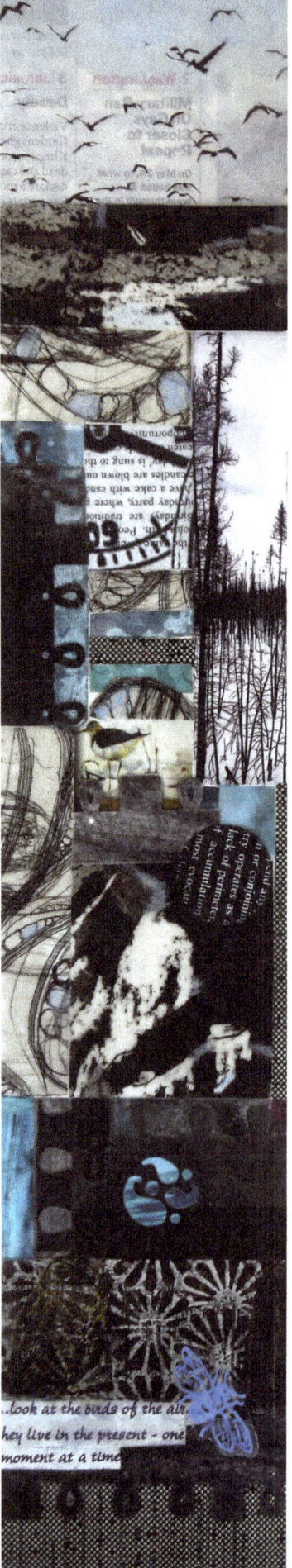

I am constantly taking photos of tree bark, not only in Virginia, but every vacation trip I ever go on. It continually amazes me that no two species have bark remotely the same. Yet patterns in nature are constantly repeated. The Fibonacci Principle—something many artists try to use in their artwork—mimics nature's repeated patterns in a consistent mathematical formula.

Live in the Present
Encaustic wax collage on wood panel
3" × 16" (8cm × 41cm)

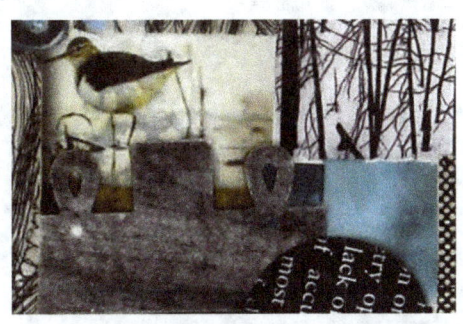

Aged paint, patterns of cracks in sidewalks, deteriorating sheds, tractors, barns, and doors, seed pods of every kind and cracked broken glass, all call my attention and keep me seeing with an artist's eye. Even photographs of man-made patterns on the inside of high-rise garage walls become fodder for my artwork. The intentional practice of paying attention to minute details that others often walk right by without noticing, keeps my visual muscles in shape.

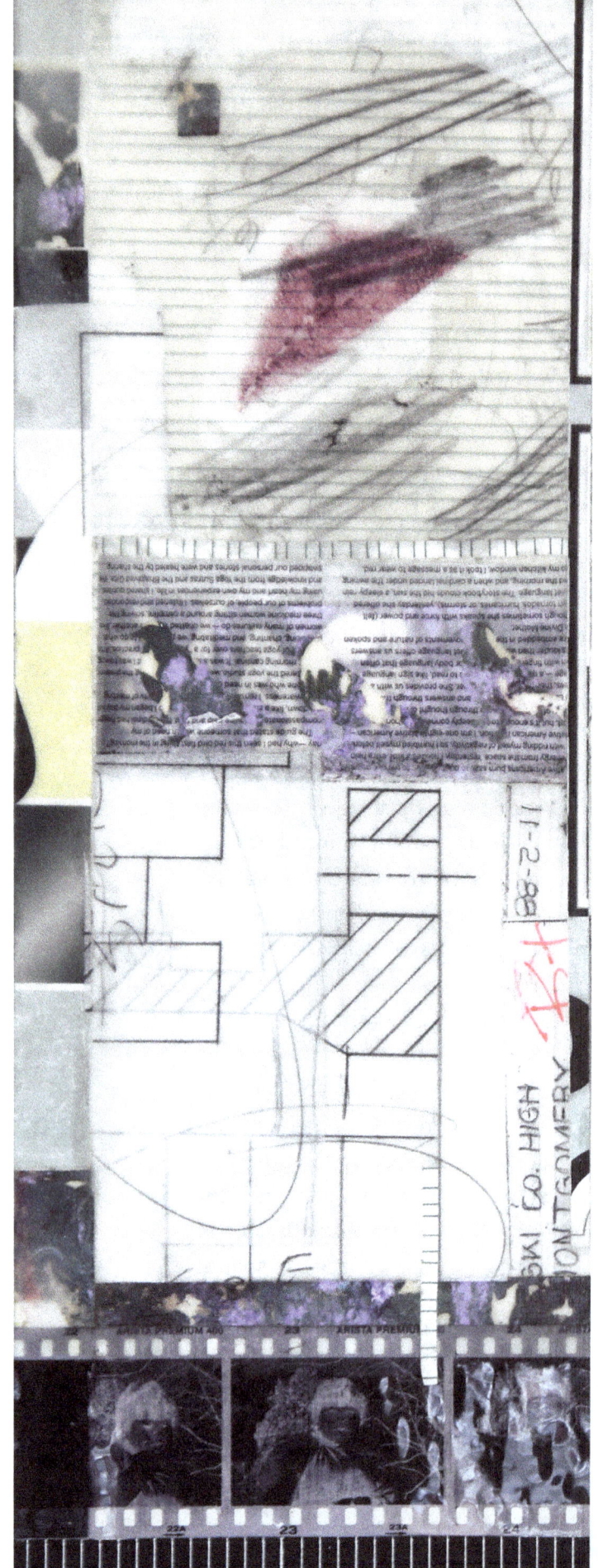

Where Did My Brother Go?
Encaustic wax collage on wood panel
4" × 10½" (10cm × 27cm)

I try to practice what the Buddhists call mindfulness, wherever I go. So the majority of inspiration for my artwork comes from the natural world first and then from other artists who are trying to express the natural world or the feelings they have about nature.

While nature is my main source of inspiration, I continue to spend a great deal of time looking at classical works as well as the work of contemporary artists. They all inspire me in different ways and for different reasons. Van Gogh for texture of the paint, Klimt for his use of pattern, Waterhouse for evoking emotion from the viewer with his romantic portrayal of women, Picasso and Braque for giving us Cubism and a totally different way of seeing things, and Renoir in how he depicted light (those grapes looked as if they could be plucked off the table. (See *An Ekphrastic Poem*, page 164).

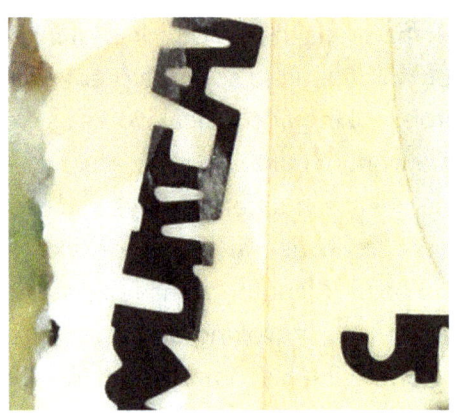 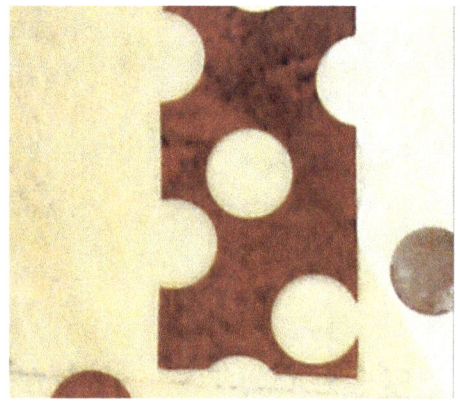

Some favorite contemporary artists who influence my work include Chuck Close for his mind boggling and systematic way of doing a portrait, Pino Daeni (born Giuseppe Dangelico), and Luis Royo for invoking atmosphere and beauty in his portraits of women.

A lot of inspiration can be found by looking at art magazines. I tear out the pages of artists' works that speak to me and add them to a binder file. I look at this file often and continually add to it. There is something to learn from every artist.

Poetry of Place
Encaustic wax collage on wood panel
4" × 19" (10cm × 48cm)

WORKING IN LAYERS

Objects can become a metaphor for the things we survive. We often can not control what happens to us but we can control our response.

In my life, I have always tried to see what good I can make of the things that happen to me. So with art, I ask myself, what can I make from discarded items to give them a second life?

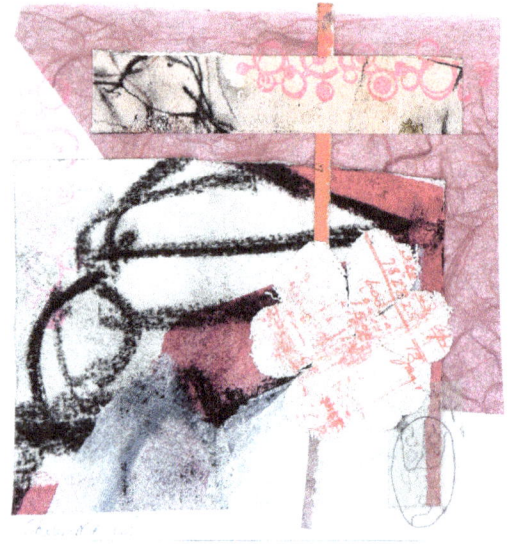

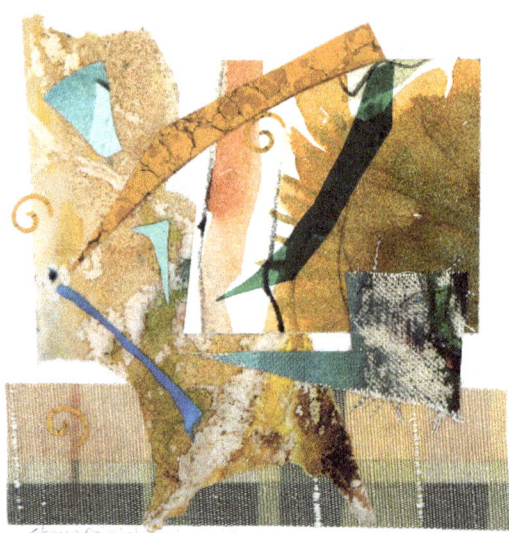

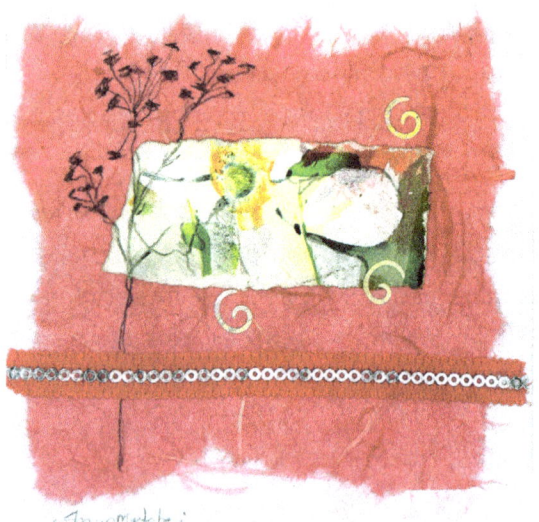

Public relations are a part of being a good business person—like it or not. As an artist, I've learned I need to promote myself and practice good business skills. Building a rapport with clients builds a relationship that could support future sales. I like to include in a heartfelt thank-you note how happy it makes me to be able to create art and that their purchase insures that I can continue to do so. I state my wish that they have as much pleasure in living with the artwork as I had in making it. These cards were made to be very personal thank-yous and to be mailed to patrons who purchased my work. I feel it is an important "professional" idea for artists to respond with courtesy when someone supports you in purchasing your work.

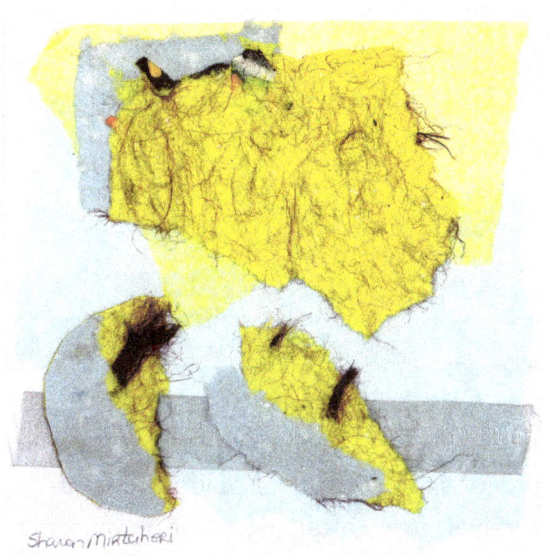
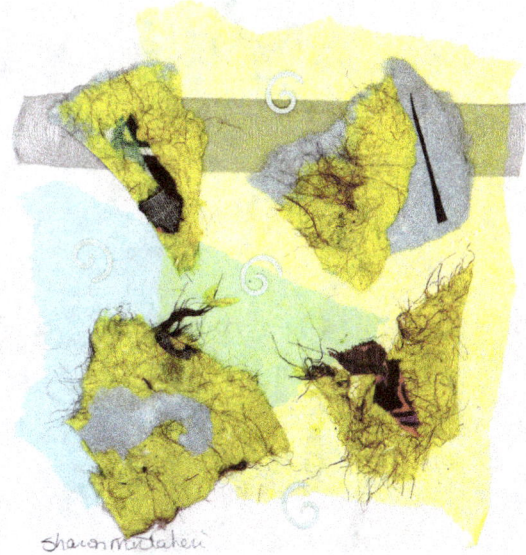
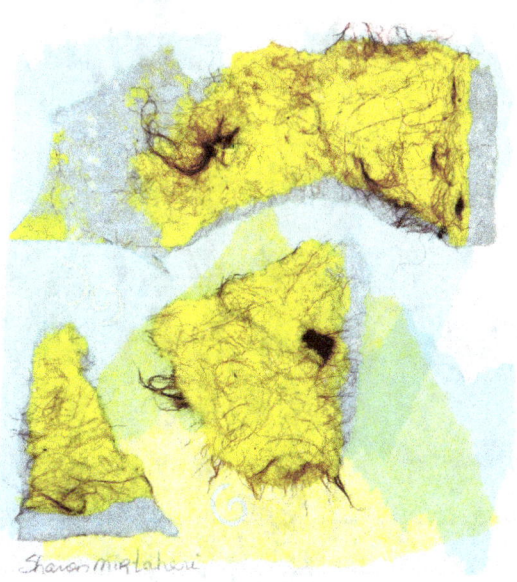

Nature is a basic theme in this body of work and is an inspirational force for me. I make strong use of natural materials and fibers in my artwork, such as: dried grasses, seed and seed heads, dried leaves of all kinds, dried and pressed flowers, thin twigs, bird feathers, and hand-made papers. The subject matter in my work borrows heavily from the arboreal and reflects a theme of growth. It is a metaphor for the spiritual and intellectual growth I have tried to pursue my entire life.

Thank-You Cards (this page and opposite)
Assorted fibrous papers and collage scraps
5" × 5" (13cm × 13cm)

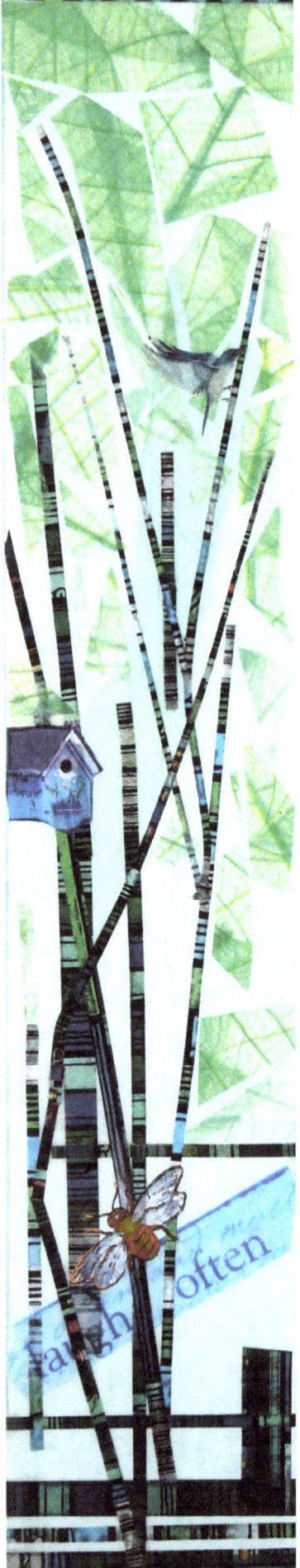

The longevity of trees symbolizes a continuity and persistence of life as well as survival. Trees often live through extreme hardships such as floods, tornadoes and wildfires. Even a scarred, contorted tree is useful providing shelter for other life forms. My repetitive use of circles mimics the growth rings of a tree and symbolizes the continuous cycles of nature. Both birds and trees are constants in the landscape over most of the earth and are images everyone can connect with. All these aspects of trees are a metaphor for my personal story.

Laugh Often
Encaustic wax collage on wood panel
3" × 16" (7cm × 41cm)

The majority of pieces I created for my thesis are vertical, narrow, wood-panel substrates of varying sizes. The wood and the vertical orientation, for me, mimics a tree form. It also reminds me of the Japanese aesthetic that I am drawn to. As an art collector who herself is out of wall space for new pieces, I also realize that everyone typically has a narrow wall somewhere in their home for a new piece of artwork.

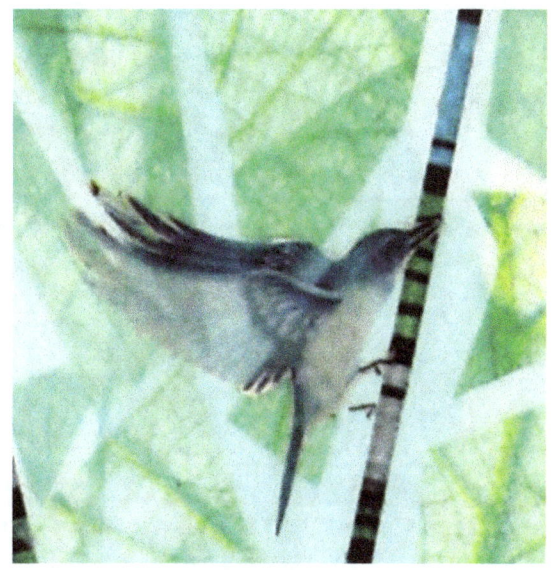

For me, the image of a bird represents that broken little girl inside who I've spent the entirety of my adult life trying to nurture and mend. I have been compelled to use birds over and over as a cathartic act. The bird represents a choice to sing mournfully or joyfully. She is a personal metaphor for choosing to be a victim or a survivor. Birds in cages, birds sitting atop cages, empty cages or structural enclosures that bring cages to mind are often images I include in my work. Cages, for me, represent being brought up in a home that was violent with no apparent escape. My childhood was filled with nightmares about snakes at every exit and no escape.

Alert
Encaustic wax collage on wood panel
5" × 9" (13cm × 23cm)

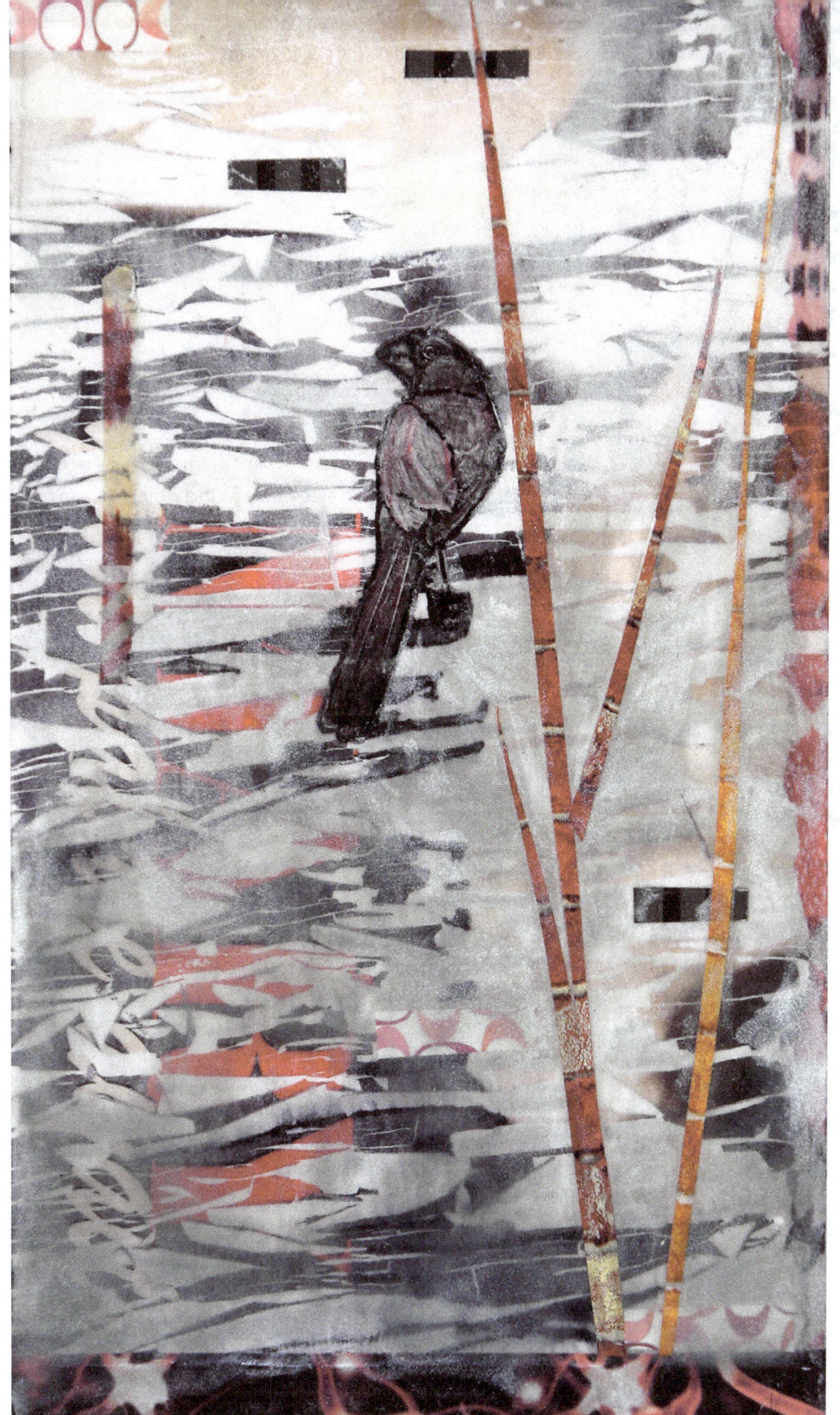

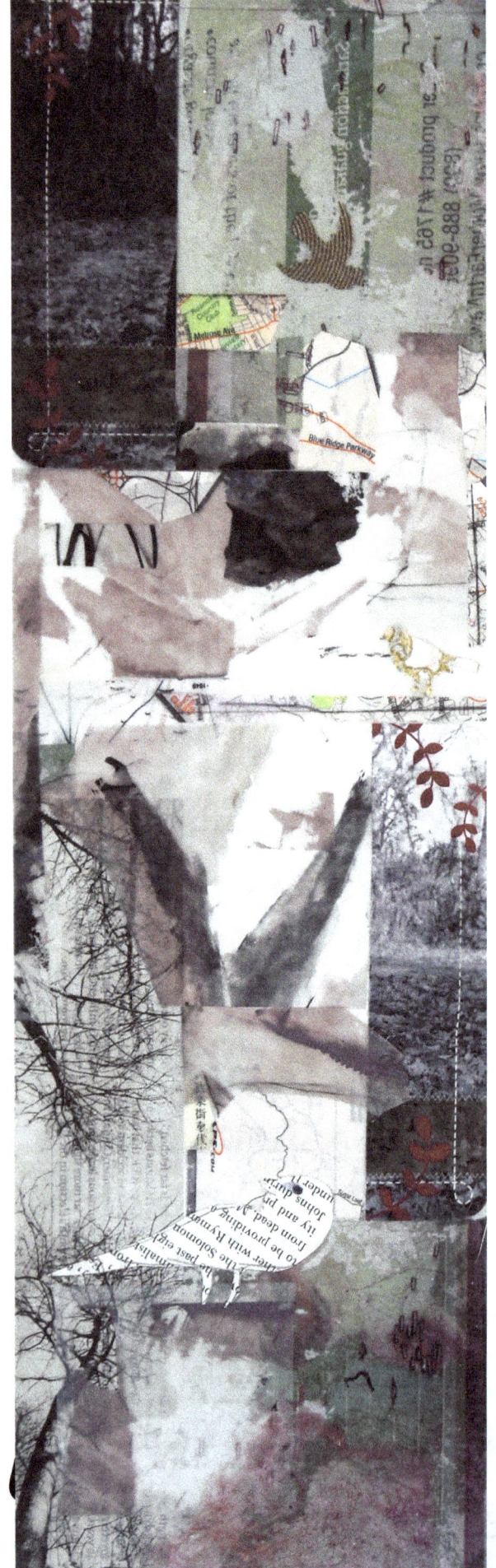

The dumpster-diver in me always wants to include as many found objects in an art piece as I can. It is a challenge I give myself. The idea of using what's been discarded and would otherwise end up in a landfill, inspires my creativity as much as nature. It tickles my muse every time. Embedded in my artwork, you will often find the following: used belt sander sheets, mis-mixed cheap paint from the hardware store, paper paint sample chips, and material from high-end upholstery fabric and wallpaper sample books.

Fly the Treetops
Encaustic wax collage on wood panel
5" × 16" (13cm × 41cm)

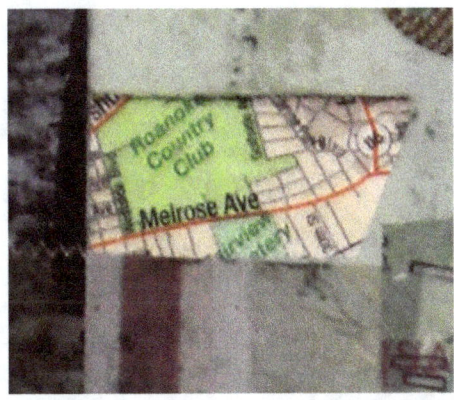

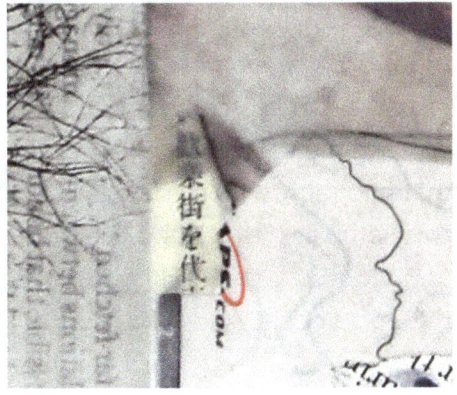

Any number of items from my own life might show up in a piece of art such as: my families old bills, receipts and bank statements, my brother's drafting homework from his high-school days, negatives of family photos, photographs themselves, vintage labels from medicines and foods, sewing pattern paper, manufacture's paper tags from clothes, scrap ribbon, old letters tea stained and printed on top of each other, and photocopies of my angst-filled diary pages from grade school. Nothing that is fairly flat escapes my scavenging or is off limits for my art work.

From other artists trashcans, I find tossed drawings, doodles, watercolors, scrap vellum, handmade papers, copper shavings from etching plates, not-up-to-snuff etchings and monotypes—all a stash of possibilities when torn up into many pieces to become interesting bits of color and texture in my own work.

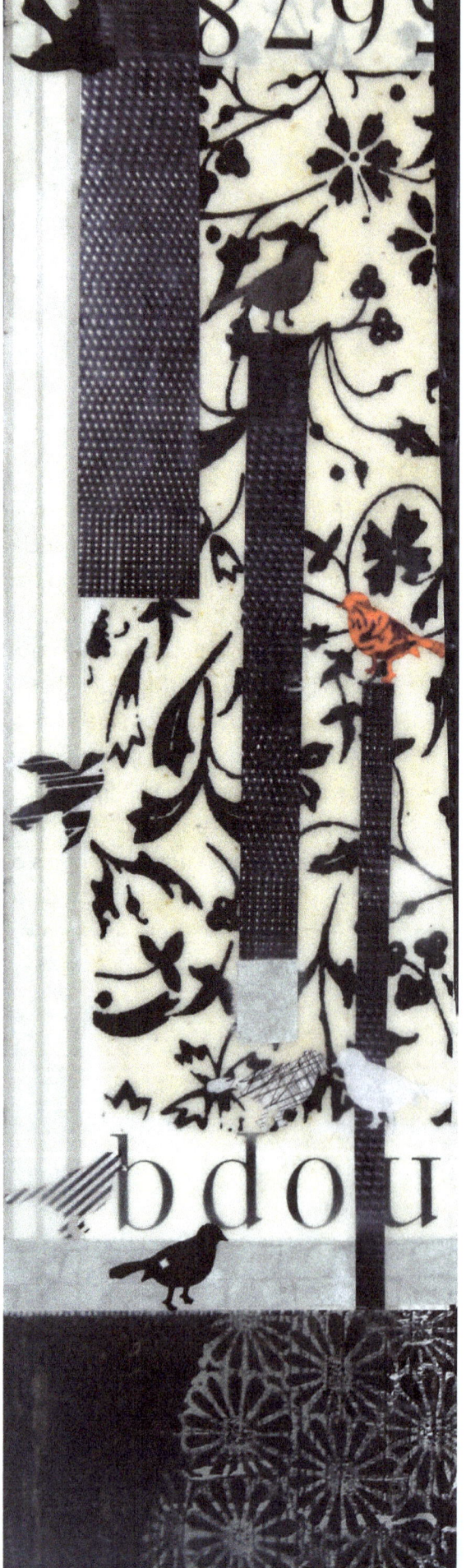

Re-appropriating is in my heritage. Grannie made quilts from old worn out bib-overalls that had holes in the seats and knees, and that had far too many patches to be useful, as well as tired dresses and blouses. She simply cut out the good parts. And, my God, my grandparents never threw anything away, ever! Fruit does not fall far from the tree.

Bird, Do You?
Encaustic wax collage on wood panel
4" × 13¼" (10cm × 34cm)

Strips of old magazine pages with texture or color that I love, worn-out books, vintage sheet music, maps, Japanese stock market newspapers, pink and yellow phone book pages, lottery tickets, movie ticket stubs, laser paper cut outs on greeting cards (great as a stencil), cocktail napkins, and gift wrap papers come together to create an enormous stash of inspiration.

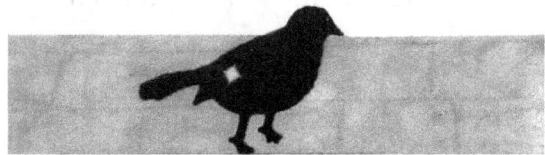

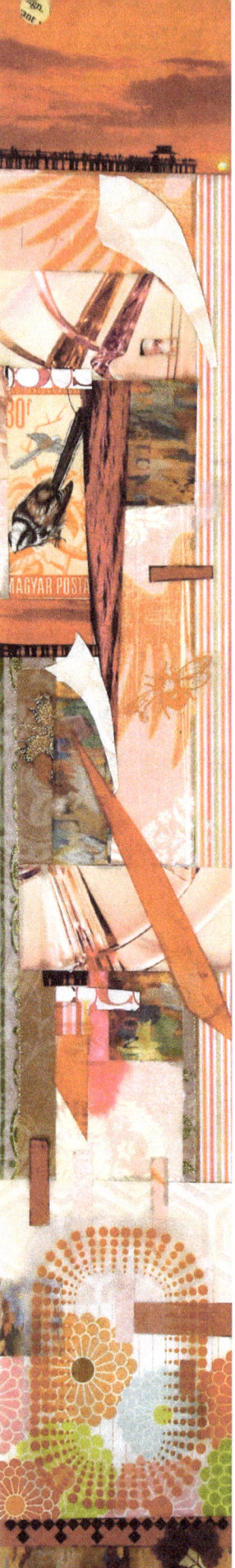

Of course there are things I actually buy to use in making art such as stamps and punches (mainly birds, leaves and trees), stencils, scrapbook papers, hand-made papers and scrapbooking stickers.

Some of the more unusual things I use are gridded dry wall tape; sewing pattern wheels that give a "ditty dot-dot" mark to wax—one of my favorite tools purchased at the fabric store; a copper pot scrubber at the dollar store that makes wonderful abstract marks; antique kitchen tools that I use to texture the warm wax surface—spatulas, for example, have all kinds of various cut-outs on them; I even found a substantial heavy gear part that I can roll over the surface of the wax and get a undulated pattern.

Fiery Sunset
Encaustic wax collage on wood panel
3" × 19" (8cm × 48cm)

There are silicone kitchen items for sale with an immense variety of patterns on them that I use in printmaking, along with plastic bath mats I get at Marshalls, TJ Max and dollar stores.

The delightful thing that happens to artists once they realize there are more uses for objects than their intended purposes is that it puts us on a fun scavenger hunt for them. Not even our spouse's tools are safe from us. It is the scavenged trash finds that excite me the most though.

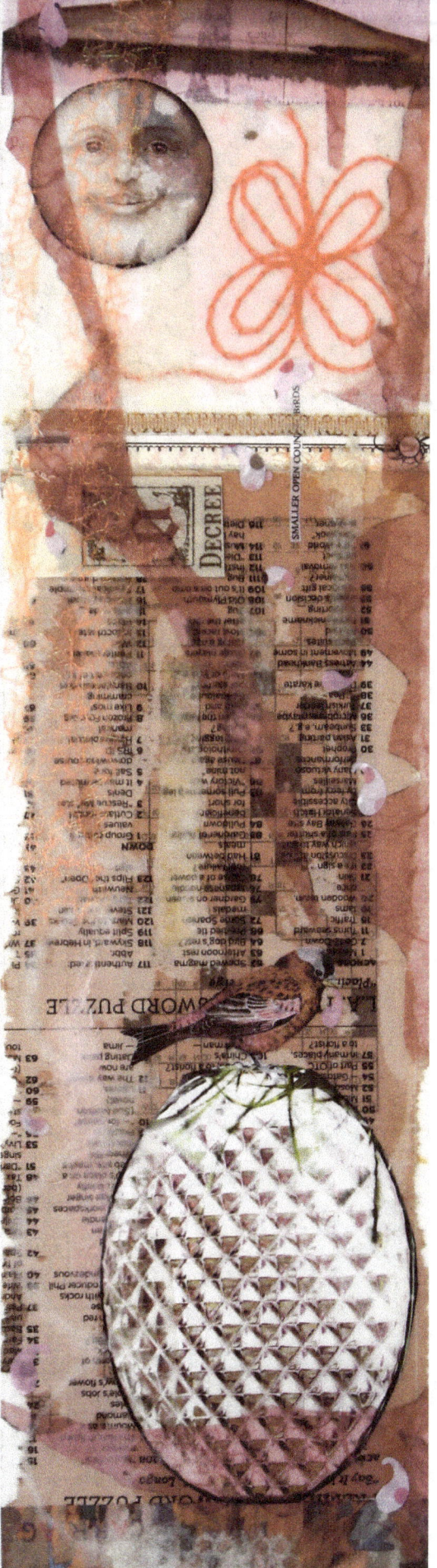

Rosy Finch Decrees it a Pink Day
Encaustic wax collage on wood panel
3½" × 15½" (9cm × 40cm)

MAKING ENCAUSTIC COLLAGE

Just about any medium can be incorporated into the magical world of encaustic collage. All of your art skills can be utilized: drawing directly onto the wax or incising it; layering such as in printmaking; embedding flat objects like collage, ethereal washes like watercolor. It will invigorate your art making and above all, you are going to have fun!

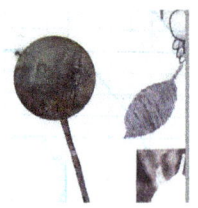 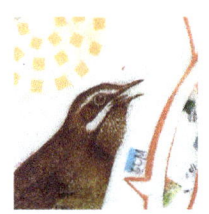 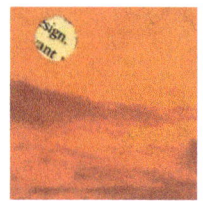 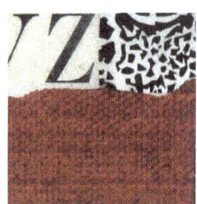 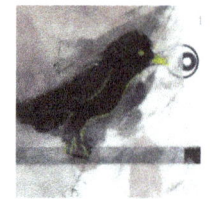

SAFETY

Before walking you through my encaustic-collage process, I must begin with some words on safety.

Encaustic wax omits harmful fumes when heated over 200°Fahrenheit. If it smokes and you breathe this in, it is dangerous. Always have *very* good ventilation. I use a small fan in a window and put my worktable directly in front of the window. I turn the fan backwards, so it pulls the air from my workspace to the outdoors. A special flat thermometer—made for encaustic work—should be kept on your hot plate at all times. Pancake griddle thermometers are not reliable. I keep a close eye on the flat thermometer, and I never turn the griddle's thermostat over 200°F.

You should always have a fire extinguisher at hand to put out any fire and a large box or two of baking soda. Wax can catch fire if water is on it or it is heated above 220°F. Also, have close at hand, a tube of burn cream. If hot wax gets on your skin, some sources suggest running cold water over the skin and wax before attempting to tear the wax off, then running more cold tap water over the burn, and then applying burn cream.

A Wagner painter's gun runs between 600°–800°F. The metal mouth stays extremely hot even after it is turned off. I now lay my gun in an aluminum pan that is slightly bigger than my heat gun. (You only have to get burned once to adhere to this safety precaution.) Yours truly placed her gun on the glass table top to have it begin to slide off the table. When I went to keep it from falling, guess which part I grabbed! Yep. I don't think those fingers have finger prints now. The R and F Paints website has an excellent safety precautions sheet that I highly recommend reading.

Some artists hold small works in one hand while fusing with the other hand. I do not recommend this practice. No matter how good you are, there is the chance your delicate inner forearm is going to "get it" eventually. Keep the art piece on the work surface and bend down to see if it is properly fused.

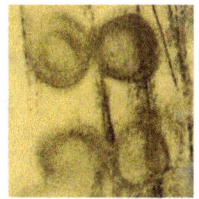 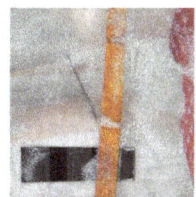 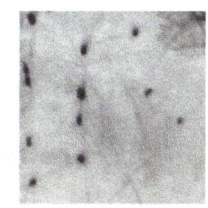 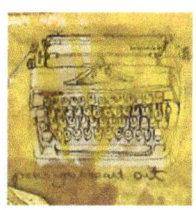 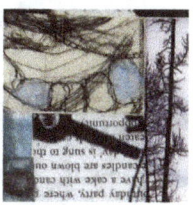

BASIC MATERIALS

This list includes the minimal supplies someone new to encaustic collage would want to gather before beginning exploration of the medium. See *Resources* (page 170) for more information.

- Beeswax (natural, unbleached) and damar crystals, or pre-mixed wax medium
- Burn cream
- Electric fans to exhaust fumes
- Encaustic hot plate or an electric pancake griddle
- Fire extinguisher
- Flat thermometer to lie on hot plate
- Heat gun (Wagner) or propane torch
- Metal spoons or ladle for adding medium to wax paints
- Metal tins—flat bottoms, various sizes, for each color of wax
- Natural bristle brushes, various sizes and shapes
- Paper towels and old rags
- Pigmented waxes (encaustic paints)
- Substrates—stiff and rigid such as wood panels, enkaustikos boards, etc.
- Tools for scraping—pointed tools, razor blades, spatula

The word *encaustic* comes from the Greek word *enkaustiko* meaning "to burn in."

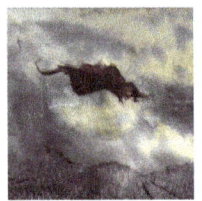 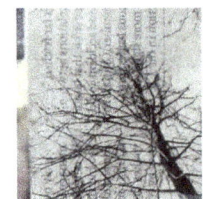 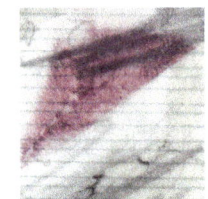 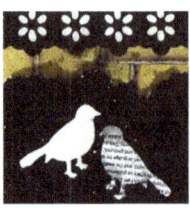 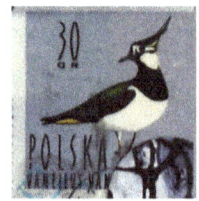

PROCESS

When I have collected and sorted through my raw materials and collected treasures, it is time to prepare mentally for creating art. This process for me includes organizing materials and tidying and cleaning up from the last session. I work in a tiny studio space (fourteen feet by seven feet) but my organizational skills make it a perfect size. I have Dollar Store plastic shoe boxes that I make into what I call my color boxes. All my finds (scavenged items, including papers), are sorted by color into these boxes. I work with a limited color palette because it keeps me focused on design principles that create harmony and unify a piece of artwork.

Substrate

A trip to a hardware store comes next for the wood substrates that I use. I buy a premium, fine-grade sheet of maple plywood and have it cut up in various skinny lengths like I prefer. While encaustic work can be done on any stiff and porous substrate, I like plywood because there is no need to frame the finished collage if the sides are treated with care. I tape off the sides with blue painters tape so the wax does not get on the sides which would make painting them later impossible. Some artists prefer to wax the sides with colored wax. I do not.

I spend a great deal of time in the preparation of the wood substrate. I sand the surface and the edges with coarse-, medium- and then fine-grit sandpaper. I find the sandpaper blocks are easier to work with. If the sides are not sanded finely, the roughness will show, even after painting them. When sanding, I try to round the edges slightly. The care taken in the crafting of the substrate pays off visually. Framing is an expensive endeavor and presenting the work as I do eliminates the need for a frame.

Many more types of rigid substrates can be used. Some examples are LuAnn board, Masonite, thin sheets of balsa wood glued to metal sheets, wood, glass or any rigid material. The reason the substrate must be rigid or stiff is the wax can crack if there is much flexibility in it. Also

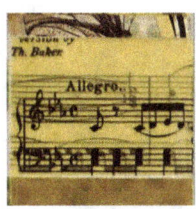 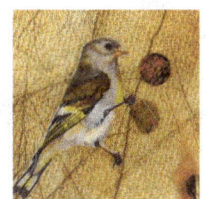 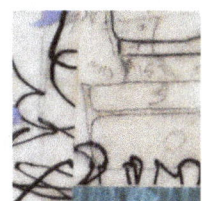 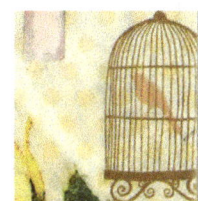 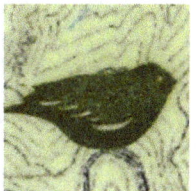

it must be porous so the wax becomes embedded in the material. This layer puts a barrier between the acidic wood and the bulk of the art work. Prepared encaustic cradle boards are the favorite of many artists and can be purchased from numerous art stores. They were developed specifically for encaustics and have deep sides (two to four inches). They are also expensive. Canvas can be used if it is glued to a stiff substrate.

Priming

I use a white acrylic primer (Kilz) as a first layer on the face of the wood panel as well as on the sides. I paint with the grain on the first layer and let it dry overnight. The second coat I apply opposite the grain. Each coat I put on as thinly as possible and use a fine natural bristle brush which minimizes brush strokes. When thoroughly dry, I sand the substrate lightly again with fine-grit sandpaper.

The next step of using a tack cloth to get off the dust is imperative as the dust will make gluing down paper very problematic. It is essential to take time to do this step well.

Gesso made by Evans Encaustics and other companies, specifically for encaustics, is available in white and several colors but it is very expensive. Although many books say encaustic paint and acrylic paint are not compatible, while oils and encaustics are, I have not had trouble with using the acrylic-based Kiltz primer. However, I do a lot of collage work first with papers. If I were to begin with wax and use only wax, I would use the gesso that is recommended.

Heat

I use Presto pancake griddles as hot plates. Presto makes a larger surface commercial pancake griddle that can be ordered online for $30–$50. I wait until they go on sale for twenty dollars and buy them. (I have eight now for when I teach workshops.) The thermostats are unreli-

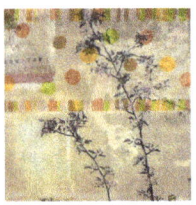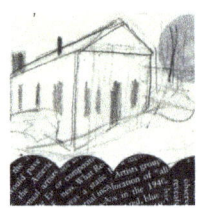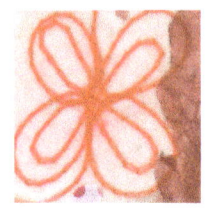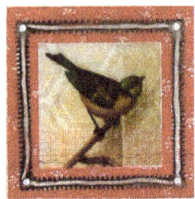

able for wax use. The center is always hotter than the outside edges, so I put larger pots in the middle and smaller ones at the edges. R and F paints sell flat thermometers that sit flush on the plate and are a must for encaustic work. Put one near the center of the plate where it gets the hottest and keep an eye on it.

Two layers of clear wax medium or two layers of colored wax are recommended as a first layer for works that are entirely done in wax. The first layer is done with the grain of the wood, the second layer opposite the grain. Heat fusing is done between each layer (more on this later).

Wax Medium

Encaustic wax medium is composed of purified beeswax and damar resin. The ratio is one part damar resin to eight parts purified beeswax. You can buy medium that comes pre-mixed with the above ratios. Many art-supply sources carry damar crystals and wax separately so you then can mix them yourself, which is less expensive. If you choose to mix the wax medium yourself, know that it is a bit difficult and time consuming. Here is the process for mixing your own medium:

Your hot plate should be cleared completely except for a container, preferably metal with a flat bottom. Damar takes a higher heat to melt completely so none of your other wax pots should be on the plate as they could smoke with the higher heat. Note that it can take up to four hours to get a large amount of damar resin to a liquid state.

I prepare the damar resin crystals by placing them in a Ziploc bag and then placing that bag inside a second Ziploc bag, pushing most of the air out of both bags as I zip them. Then I wrap the bags inside a beach towel. I place it on my concrete basement floor and use a hammer to smash the crystals into a powder. I make large batches of powder-ized damar at a time when I do this and then just measure out the "one part damar" ratio when I want to make a mix. I use tablespoon-measurements, but some artists make huge batches of medium at a time.

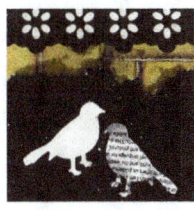 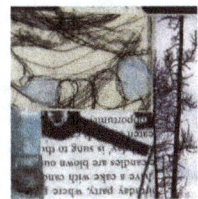 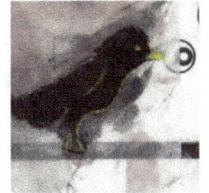 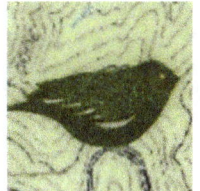 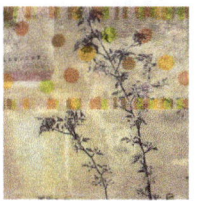

I measure out one part of the eight parts bees wax and the one part damar resin and place them in a metal baking loaf pan. I start with the thermostat at 200°. I use a large metal spoon and push the crystal powder to the bottom and try to stir it in with the melting beeswax. The crystals are very sticky and the goal is to get them to melt and incorporate into the fluid of the beeswax. I inch up the heat gradually until I see it melting. I never go over 220°F. If it begins to smoke at all I turn back the thermostat immediately.

When the damar is fully incorporated into the wax, I turn back the thermostat to 200. You must wait until the flat thermometer on your hot plate shows that it is at 200° before you add the rest of the wax. This process will take at least an hour—more if you do large batches.

After it is melted, pour the wax through a paper paint strainer (from the hardware store) to filter out the various bee parts from the wax container and debris from the damar resin powder. Have a container ready for the medium. I use baking loaf pans because they do not take up all of the space on the pancake griddle.

Pigmented Wax

Pigmented wax can come in many shapes and sizes: pellet form, sticks, and bars. The bars and sticks can be shaved with a grater into a flat tin, or simply melted in a tin, whole. The colors come in various densities of opaqueness from translucent to completely opaque. Evans Encaustics has a line of pearlized pigments and metallic pigments which are divinely delicious. An opaque pigment can be made more translucent by adding a larger ratio of encaustic medium than pigment.

You can also buy a set of primary colors and mix your own colors of pigmented wax, which can save you a lot of money.

Some artists buy their own pure pigment powders and mix into the purified beeswax themselves. Be aware that the fine particulates of these pigments can be very dangerous and require the use of an appropriate respirator. Many pure

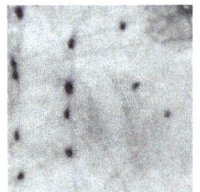 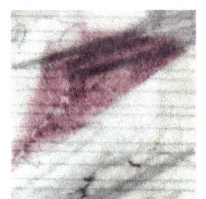 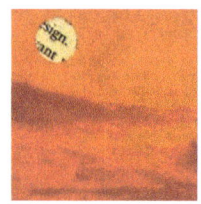 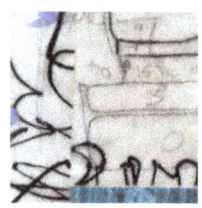 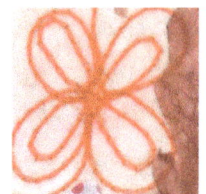

Wax-Mixing Ratios		
Powderized Damar Resin Crystals		Purified Beeswax
1 ounce	to	8 ounces (½-lb)
2 ounces	to	16 ounces (1-lb)
4 ounces	to	32 ounces (2-lbs)
8 ounces	to	64 ounces (4-lbs)

*Any measuring devise will work as long as the ratio is **one part damar resin to eight parts wax**, either in powder form, pellet, or flake. Powder is easier to measure.*

pigments are toxic. I say, be kind to your lungs and just shell out the extra money for the pigmented waxes.

Containers for holding melted wax atop the hot plate need to be perfectly flat on the bottom to maintain an even heat; otherwise you will have some wax melted and some semi-solid in the pan. Empty, clean tuna cans do not work as they have an elevated metal rim around the periphery. R and F Paints sell tin containers that are flat and printmaking supply companies sell empty tin containers for holding inks which also work very well. I have found some at the Dollar Store that are flat and some that were not. The ones that were not have lids and the lids are flat. While shallow, they work well for small batches

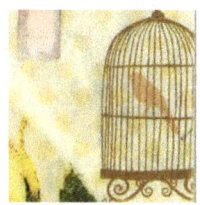 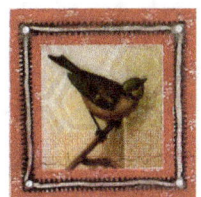 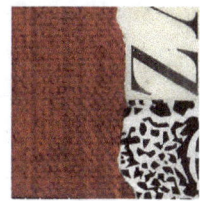 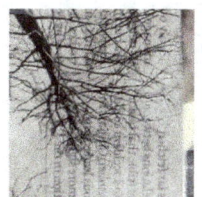 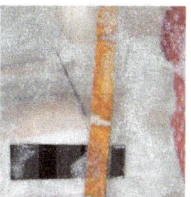

of wax. Many shapes and sizes of cake baking pans that are flat work well. Flea markets and antique stores are sources for pancake griddles and old pans. Add those to the list of best-friend places for wax artists.

The tin containers get hot when in use, so use caution when moving them around on the hot plate or off the plate. I use two or more wooden clothes pins on my small tins to lift them off. For the heavier and bigger metal containers, I use rubber handled metal pliers to grab the edges of the containers and move them around the hot plate or to take them off the hotplate. Clothes pins and metal binder clips work well to keep the brushes from drowning in the pots of wax.

Application

Wax may be applied to the substrate in many ways. One can use a brush to paint the wax onto the substrate. Natural bristle brushes in any size or shape can be utilized for this method (nylon/man-made materials tend to melt in the hot wax).

Small thin brushes work well for making lines or filling in areas with color. Large flat brushes work best for laying down medium over the entire surface. Japanese Hake brushes work well if you desire the smoothest surface. Inexpensive natural brushes from a hardware store also work, although you get a slightly coarser surface than with the Hake brushes. If a coarse surface is unwanted it can be minimized in the fusing of the surface.

Working with brushes means there is a window of mere seconds before the wax cools and hardens. This is the most challenging trait of encaustic wax for most artists and one that must be dealt with by having vast amounts of patience.

The brush can be laid directly on the hot plate for re-melting the wax or placed on the bottom of the tin container you are working with for a minute or so to allow the hardened wax to re-melt. Keep in mind that any brush you use in wax can never be used for anything else, including other types of painting. On the upside, there is no need to clean your brushes like

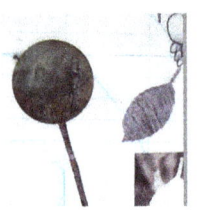 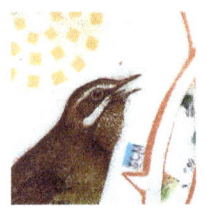 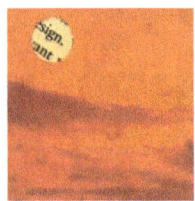 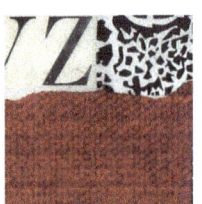 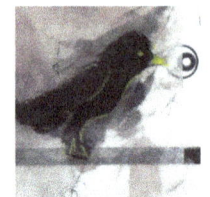

you have to do for other types of painting. Simply let them harden and leave them in the color wax tins or the container you have for medium.

I dedicate one brush for each color of wax. If you do not want to invest in that many brushes, you can simply melt the wax off on the hot plate and wipe the brushes quickly with paper towels until most of the wax if removed, then use the brush again. Tools can be cleaned in the same manner.

Wax can be dripped or poured directly onto the substrate as well. When poured, make sure to have a waxed-paper lined pan underneath to be able to reuse wax that drips off.

Other Applications

Many art supply companies sell encaustic wax supplies (refer to suppliers list at the end of the book), and encaustic tools, substrates, (including cradled boards specifically for encaustics), pigmented wax and pre-made medium. With growing popularity for encaustic painting specialized tools have been invented in last few decades for encaustic wax artists. Some of these hold the wax in a pencil-like device and keep it melted as you apply it to the substrate. Some artists do portraits of a fine realistic quality with such tools. (Vicki Alderman, a UK artist, does the best encaustic portraits I have ever seen outside a museum.)

There are tacking irons which work to smooth and fuse the surface. When you turn the tacking iron sideways, you can use the edge to push the wax around on the surface. Encaustic sculpting artists make good use of this method. Some inventive artists even use a household iron and miniature quilting irons.

Fusing

Fusing tools are very important in this medium because each layer of wax put down must be fused to the layer beneath it to ensure the layers do not come apart or flake off. Every time you fuse, you melt each layer to the one before. The heat tools used for this fusing range from

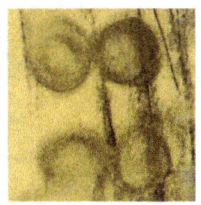 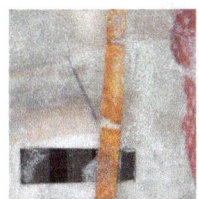 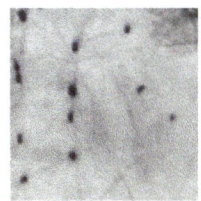 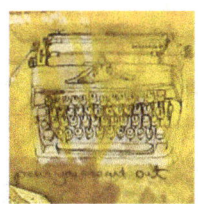 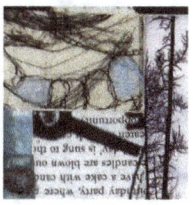

painters' heat guns to crème brûlée torches with disposable butane cartridges, to welder's torches. The crème brûlée torch gives a small pinpoint heat source which is good if you want to fuse a small area without disturbing the area around it. The painter's heat gun has a fairly wide nozzle and does a bigger area at a time. I must be honest; I bought the crème brûlée torch and I have never used it. (An open flame gives me the heebie-jeebies.) Use what you are most comfortable with.

When fusing with a painter's heat gun or with a torch, it is important to be at least 4" (10cm) from the surface. You are looking for the dull surface of the cooled wax to turn shiny. Keep the heat source moving either in long strokes over the length of the surface or in concentric circles. Once you see the shine, fusing is complete. If the heat source is left in one spot too long the wax will turn to liquid again, which is not necessary.

If the wax is thicker in one spot or over the entire piece than you prefer, you can tilt the piece over wax paper and apply the heat source in circles until the wax become liquid and runs off the substrate. (I elevate the piece on a slotted kitchen shelf riser, from Bed Bath and Beyond, and put wax paper underneath it.) You can peel off the wax and reuse it this way. I do this when I have an embedded object for which I want the details to show clearly.

A second option for removing excess wax is to scrape it off using a razor blade held at a 45° angle. Some artists use this scraping technique to get very interesting surfaces when they have applied two or more colors of wax. A ceramicist's loop tool also works well for removing unwanted wax. After any scraping, I fuse lightly again to even out the surface.

Composition

Monotypes

Monotypes can be made using encaustic wax. A hot griddle is employed with various types of acid free papers (thin Japanese printmaking paper for example).

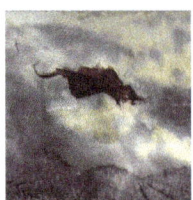 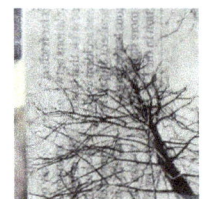 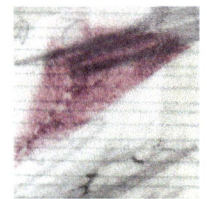 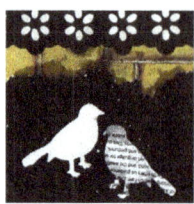 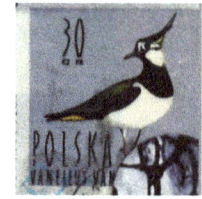

Colored pigmented wax bars or sticks are used directly on the paper which lies on the surface of the griddle. This is akin to an immediate-drawing method. The wax can be moved on the surface of the paper or removed by scrapping it off with various tools as long as it lies on the griddle. The paper will eventually become saturated through and through and at that point one can no longer add wax. Each type of paper has a different saturation point but in general, the thinner the paper the quicker the paper becomes saturated. Thin paper has a certain luminosity that I love.

Paula Roland invented a griddle in which the paper can be registered, but again, this is expensive. I use a twenty dollar pancake griddle from a department store but there is no way to register easily.

Paper will only absorb so much wax. Every kind of paper has a different absorption amount. In my need not to waste wax, I discovered that if there was a little bit of wax on the plate I could lay thin Japanese papers down to absorb the wax creating a lovely translucent layer. It is a great way to start out with a sterile white sheet. Making that first mark can be intimidating for some artists.

Because paper is thin and can't really be displayed on the wall without glass and framing, I prefer to mount finished monotypes in a floating fashion on white mat board with old-fashioned, clear photo triangles. The scrapbooking section of most craft stores carries them. The reason for the use of the triangle photo holders is that the wax-saturated paper will not adhere to mat board with other methods of hinging.

Layering

The use of encaustic wax is not unlike the layering of sheer inks in the monotype process. Items laid in the first layer of wax, deeply embedded, show form and less detail. The objects near the surface clearly show details. There is no limit to how many layers of wax one can use as long as the substrate is stiff and rigid. Some wax artists create sculpture with the wax.

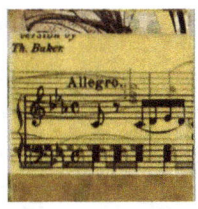 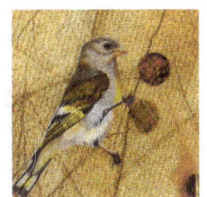 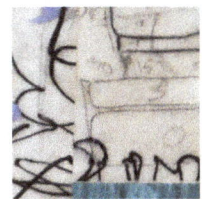 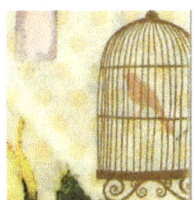 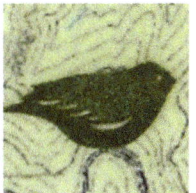

Encaustic wax can have an ethereal, luminous quality when pigmented wax is used sparingly with a higher ratio of wax medium. This quality is my favorite aspect of encaustic wax. When heavily-pigmented colored wax is used with very little wax medium, a more opaque result happens. It is then more like using oil paint. This versatility in expression of density of color is very alluring and seductive.

Wax Removal

Just as important to the finished piece is the possibility of removing wax versus adding it. There are many common tools one can use to accomplish this removal with. A few are: razor blades, X-Acto knives, nails of various sizes, screws of various sizes (gives a ragged edge to the line and the ragged edge can be removed with the razor blade if undesired), ice picks, metal nail cuticle pushers, printmaking tools, and ceramics tools. Any metal household items such as spatulas or grill top hand-held scrapers can be used. Plastic tools are not a good idea as they can't be heated to remove wax without melting.)

Interesting patterns can be made by scraping the surface of several built up colors on a substrate with an angled razor blade. It gives a look of aged paint on furniture that has been painted many colors over a period of time. You can go as deeply as removing two colors in some areas or three or more in other areas.

If you want control of what is removed keep the razor blade clean by carefully pulling off the wax. It you don't remove the wadded-up wax on the razor blade it can redeposit the color in other places (sometimes a happy accident). I always keep the removed wax in a separate tin for interesting new color pots.

To clean the razor blades of wax simple lay them on your hot plate and remove from the plate with needle nose pliers, then wipe on a rag or paper towel.

One of my favorite things that can be done with sharp pointed tools is incising the wax for the purpose of drawing on

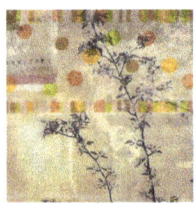 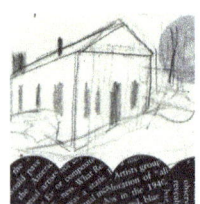 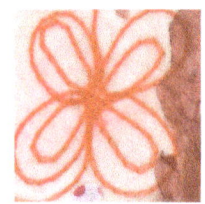 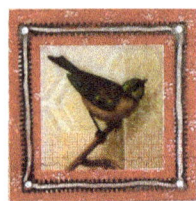 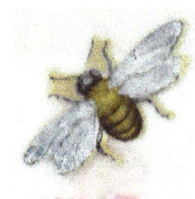

top of either clear of colored wax. When incising is finished, you can make the lines really stand out by using oil paint sticks or oil pastels. Two methods work:

Run the oil stick over the lines or if you cannot get the line filled in totally (and that is what you want), use a gloved finger to push the paint into the line. Afterward, use a small amount of canola oil on a paper towel and remove as much of the excess paint from the surface of your wax design as you like. When some paint is left on the surface you can get delicate stains of paint in other areas, which I often like. If a hard line is desired just remove all of the surface paint. Then wipe with clean paper towels several times to remove the canola oil from the wax surface. One of my favorite incising tools is a sewing pattern transfer devise. I am not sure what they call them in sewing but it is similar to a roulette tool in printmaking. It has a handle with a toothed metal wheel. When it is run over the surface of the wax it imparts small, intermittent dash lines. I use the oil stick to make the dashes obvious and have even drawn flowers and leaves on the surface with them.

Another unusual tool for incising the surface is a metal pot cleaner scrubber. They have coils of very thin metal wire and it makes a circular pattern on the surface of the soft wax.

I also collect, from antique stores, wooden carved batik stamps. I use these on the surface of the wax when it is still warm to impress a pattern on the surface. They clean up well by heating up the surface with the heat gun until the wax melts off. Metal cookie cutters also make an impression in warm wax. I have a collection of antique ones and some contemporary ones. They come in hundreds of shapes, even animal shapes.

Anytime you incise the surface of the wax and use oil sticks you then have to add a layer of clear medium and fuse. If you do not do this, whatever your next step is can blur, smear, or remove the oil paint form the lines.

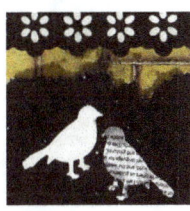 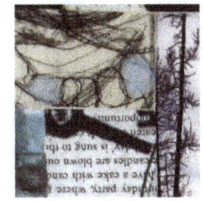 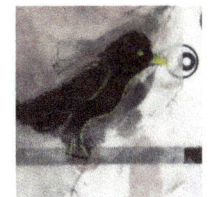 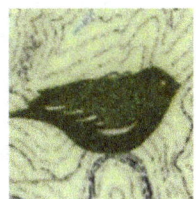 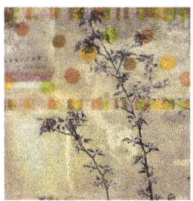

Stencils

Another design method is using stencils to build up wax on the surface. You can use store bought stencils, hand-made stencils, embossing metal plate stencils, plastic packing material that has a cut out design (love this up-cycling! One more use before it hits the landfill). To reuse stencils (if they are heatproof), lay them on the hot plate and wipe off excess wax. For non-heatproof stencils, put them in the freezer for ten minutes and the cold wax pops right off. I also use the negative, left over cardboard that has punch-out items for scrapbooking. It is often called chipboard and comes in sheets you push out. Borders for scrapbooking often have designs in them that are punched out too. The most unusual thing I use as a stencil is a tape used in plastering walls that is found in hardware stores.

Two back-to-back layers of blue painters' tape can make a substrate for a stencil. Cut it out in desired pattern or lines on a self-healing mat. If you want to avoid an area, taping off with painter's tape is the best way to do that.

Areas that have been stenciled can be hand colored with oil pastels. Use the canola-oil-rubbing-off method described on the previous page to produce lovely detail work leaving the color in the lows and removing it in the highs of the mini sculpture.

The hardware store is going to be as good a friend to you as an encaustic wax artist as is the scrapbooking section of a craft store. Go in with new eyes!

Drawing

It is possible, if you love to draw, to do a very detailed drawing on three or four coats of clear wax medium. Just follow the instructions for laying medium down as a primer. If you want a white background, glue a piece of white printmaking paper to the wood panel first. I do a lot of drawing and stamping on vellum, parchment, or transparent papers. The paper tends to disappear when waxed over with

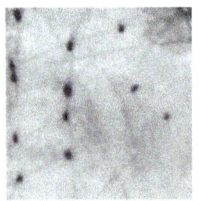 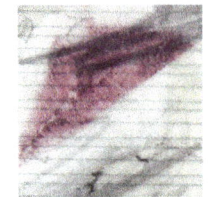 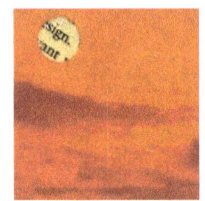 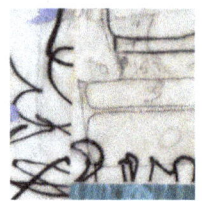 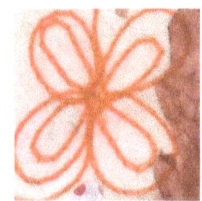

clear medium. If I do not want to see the paper at all I cut out around the edges of the drawing. When drawing directly on the wax surface with pencil, charcoal or permanent marker, you have to carefully put a coat of clear wax medium over it in order to keep it from smearing or running, and fuse very lightly. I have used wax pencils with more success and although it can be a tricky endeavor, it is worth the effort.

Image Transfer

Making image transfers is another exciting possibility on a wax surface. There are many methods, but the one I have found to be the easiest with wax is as follows. Duplicate the image you want to work with on a black-and-white toner copier. (Keep in mind it will be backwards upon transfer unless you use the mirror image function on the copier.) Make any size you desire by enlarging it or shrinking it on the copier. I usually do it in numerous sizes so as to have a choice at hand when I am ready to create the artwork.

The waxed surface should be warm to the touch, not melted. Simply run the heat gun over it once quickly. Lay the copy on the surface right side down and burnish the back entire surface of the paper with a metal spoon. You can use a credit card, metal spoon, or any kind of scraper so the paper makes good contact with the wax. Make sure to do this to the edges so you do not lose any of the image. Take your time and be thorough. Spritz the back of the paper with water from a water sprayer until it is damp. Then rub your fingers in small circles until you rub the paper backing off. You might have to reapply water several times if bits are not coming off when you rub or the paper dries out.

The toner from the copy should stay on the wax surface. This takes time and patience. If there is a film on the wax surface when the paper is rubbed off, spritz and rub again until most of the paper is removed. This film will generally disappear when the clear coat medium is applied next and fused. There are other methods of transfer that I have not tried yet.

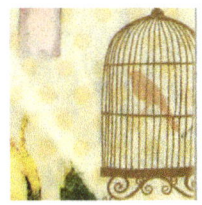 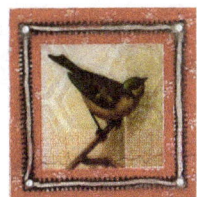 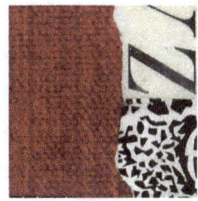 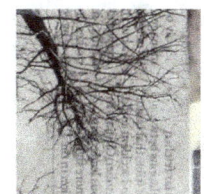 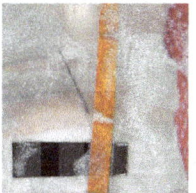

Finishing

At the very end of the creating process, I paint the sides either black or white, depending on the majority of color on the surface and what harmonizes best with that color. Occasionally I will paint the sides a color to coordinate with a composition.

Hanging Hardware

The hanging mechanics I prefer are small eye screw hooks and braided picture-framing wire. I place the eyes screws down one-fourth of the total height of the piece, and 1/4" (6mm) in from the sides. For a final touch, I use black electrical tape wound neatly around the area of the braided wire that is wrapped around itself which protects both the wall it will hang on as well as the hands of the one doing the hanging. (The frayed ends of the wire can be sharp.) Details count! I use this method on all my pieces as I have found them to hang best and most evenly with this measurement ratio.

As you can see there are so many different techniques for encaustic wax. The medium is über versatile and forgiving. When reheated items can easily be removed, the only limitation is your imagination.

LAYERS OF DESIGN

It is good to know what positive and negative attributes you have in making art. My dyscalculia bleeds over into my drawing skills especially when angles are involved. I can draw using gradations of color more easily than drawing a direct line. I have a keen eye for color shift, likely from doing hair color for thirty years. Drawing is useful but if you're not great at it, it does not mean you can't be artistic.

There's a lot of value for an artist to build an intimate relationship with the materials he or she works with and to continually strive to master the nuances of the medium they work in. This can take a lifetime.

Throughout my journey of discovery with encaustic collage, I have found I love to use the hide-and-reveal quality of the wax as a metaphor for memory. Some memories are fuzzy and some—such as violence—are hauntingly clear. You can see this used throughout the art in this book; aspects of memory, its gaps, fuzziness, and sometimes frightening clarity.

Metaphors, symbols, re-appropriating, knowledge of tools, and experimentation all play key roles in encaustic wax creations, but when all is said and done, one must generally apply art design principles for a successful work of art.

When I began my studies at Hollins, I came to the table with a deficiency in drawing as well as the knowledge of art design principles. My last undergraduate class was Senior Seminar, and Jan Knipe was my professor. I was honest with her at the very beginning and told her I had never had a class in design and that sometimes what I would create was good but that often it was not. It was hit and miss.

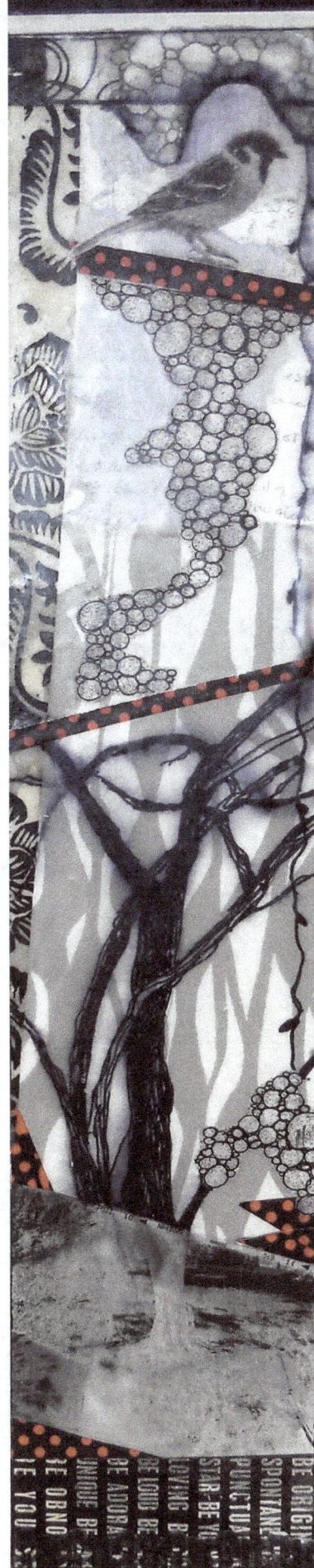

Be
Encaustic wax collage on wood panel
3" × 16" (8cm × 41cm)

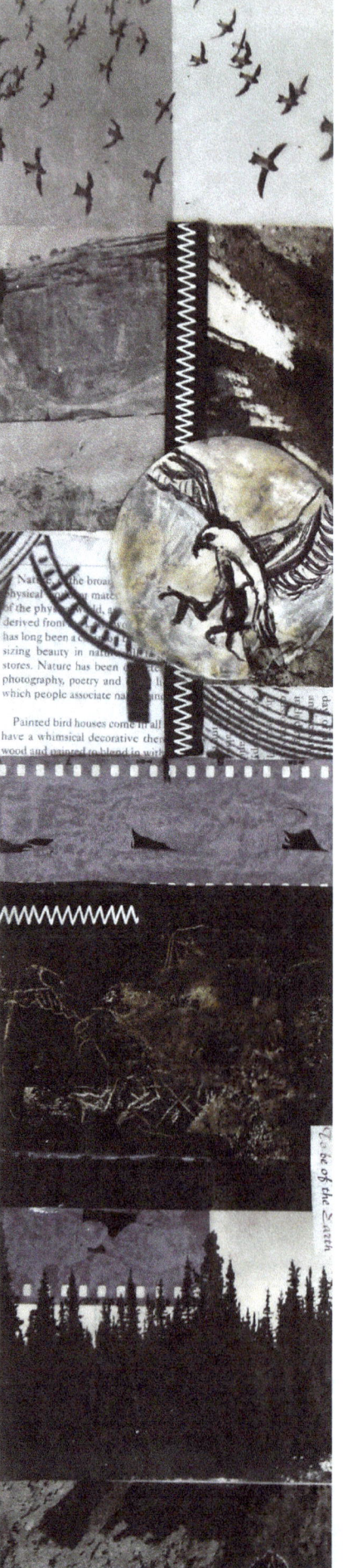

Raven
Encaustic wax collage on wood panel
3½" × 15½" (9cm × 39cm)

I did not know the design principles one needs as an artist and I understood this very well after four years at Hollins. I asked her if she could help me in this area, and, she did. Every time I now sit down to do an art piece, I hear her words in my head and I am indebted to her for sharing her knowledge of design with me.

While I did learn many helpful bits of information from Knipe's tutelage, I know there is more for me to learn. Because I am a bit weaker in the area of art design principles, I purposefully work in a limited color palette and on a small scale. This forces me to really concentrate on design principles. Limiting myself narrows the possibilities and keeps me from becoming distracted. I am slowly working larger as my skills improve. Most of the works in this book are in black, white and grey, with small bits of bright color, or in various tones of one color. I love color but do not feel I am at a point where I can work across the color wheel.

I focus on the design principles of layering (the printmaker in me does this and it lends itself perfectly to encaustic wax), and repetition. Sometimes it is the images that are repeated and sometimes it is the color or shapes. I keep myself aware of where the eye travels and repetition keeps the eye moving over the canvas, not off the canvas.

The brain automatically seeks out "like things" (if you are interested in brain functions and vision I highly recommend you read *Scientific American Mind* magazine). The brain constantly tries to label objects even in an abstract work which is perhaps why non-artists get frustrated with works of abstract art. The brain continually fills in gaps that are not actually seen. This function makes it difficult to learn to draw as you have to override this function in order to draw only what is seen. Repetition works as a type of rhythm or visual music, making movement in the artwork.

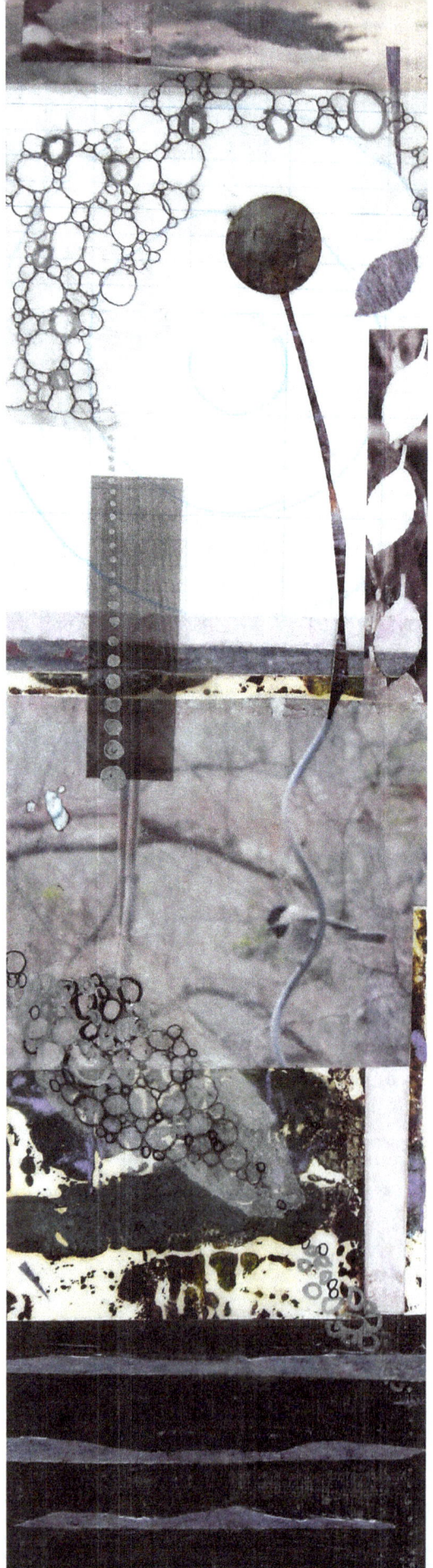

Black-Capped Chickadee
Encaustic wax collage on wood panel
4½" × 16" (10cm × 41cm)

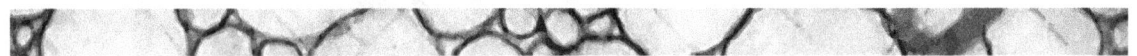

I try to be aware of what lines, shapes, texture and color are doing in a piece. Diagonals become pointers and draw the eye around the canvas. It makes a piece of art work more dynamic. I admit I am not as confident using diagonals, and my goal is to use them more often as my skills improve. Questions I ask myself often are: Are the lines varied? What is the quality of the line? Are they having a conversation? Do they make a pattern?

One also has to be aware of the positive as well as the negative spaces. The in-between objects and shapes can be as interesting, if not more interesting, than the main objects and shapes themselves. Negative space can work as a place for the eye to rest.

I'm always tempted to add more and so sometimes I need to work against my nature to keep from making a piece too busy. I ask myself: Are there places for the eye to rest? Where are they? When have I said enough? When is it finished?

I had to learn the answer to this last question a long time ago after beauty school. Watching other perfectionist hairstylists completely ruin a great cut by going over and over it, taught me too much is not a good thing!

I ask myself questions such as: Is there variety, unity, balance? I prefer the Japanese aesthetic of slightly-off-balance, and also the Fibonacci principal mentioned earlier.

I use standard shapes such as circles, squares and triangles but just as often use hand-cut odd shapes that are not recognizable. My favorite is an oval-like shape with a long skinny tail that curls slightly at the end. Think spermatozoa or paisley. These odd shapes are fresh to the eye of a viewer—new and interesting.

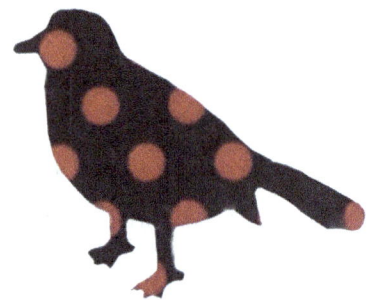

There is always a personal narrative in my artwork. It is one of the things that inspires me, but it is not necessary for the viewer to know this narrative in order to enjoy the art. I have as much fun naming my work as I do creating it. It can be a very creative thing in itself actually. Often I give a hint of the narrative in the title but I sometimes just use something that is in the work itself, such as the name of a bird in the stamp used, or if there is text I sometimes use that or part of the text. One of my favorite titles in the past was "The Language of Trees." I tried to show in a somewhat abstract fashion where trees lived and what they did without showing trees themselves.

Professor Bill White had us read a very dated and dry book by Harold Speed titled: *The Science and Practice of Drawing*. As difficult as its Old English was to read, in the end, I totally understood why he chose it. If you could get past the antiquated language it had some meaty pearls of art wisdom in it. I cannot find the book in my library, but I remember one thing Speed talked about vividly as it was an ah-ha moment. It was the word "dither," which I took to mean the serendipity and tension in a piece of artwork. The non-perfection aspects of happy accidents work as "dither." If it does not happen by accident I try to intentionally include it. Instead of a straight line I might make a jagged line. This tension or "dither" acts as a wake-up shake to the viewer. A juxtaposition of contrasts also works as "dither." For example an upside down bird.

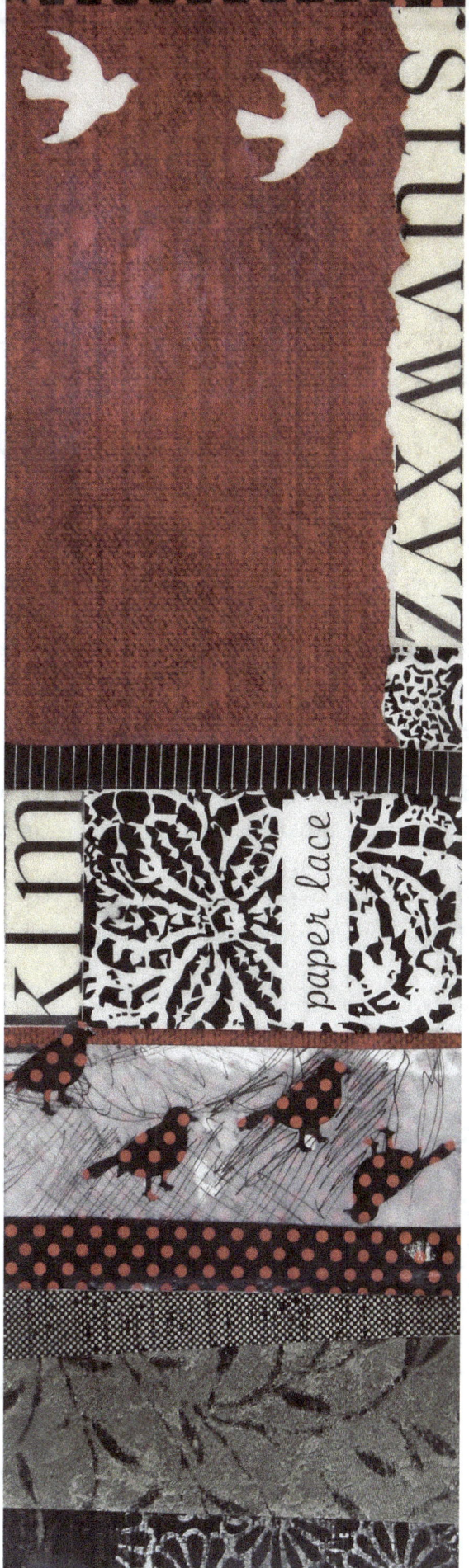

Feeling a Little Upside Down? Care to do the Polka?

Encaustic wax collage on wood panel
4" × 13" (10cm × 33cm)

I am a type-A personality tending toward seeking perfection. That trait worked against me in creating art until I realized that when I wanted to "fix" something that is exactly when I should step back and ask questions. Most of the time that very thing is just what I should leave alone otherwise the artwork can become sterile. Does that drip in the wax add "dither" or not? Do those two things not lining up add interest or distract the viewer? Do those objects not matching up create a hole that is bothersome or do they bring something magical? Those little accidents that work against "visual perfection" are often what make a work of art exciting.

In a speech at Hollins University, Fiona Ross spoke about her body of work entitled "Walking the Parallels to Terminus" and said something to this effect: Mistakes saved her from the poverty of her intentions. When examining the natural world closely it becomes apparent that nothing is perfect or uniform. Trees never grow straight as they seek the sun which moves from morning to night and from season to season. My living room window gets sun in the summer but the sun never shines through it in winter. Why should humans or artists try to make things perfect when nature has not? So at last my perfectionism is working for me in a type of reverse.

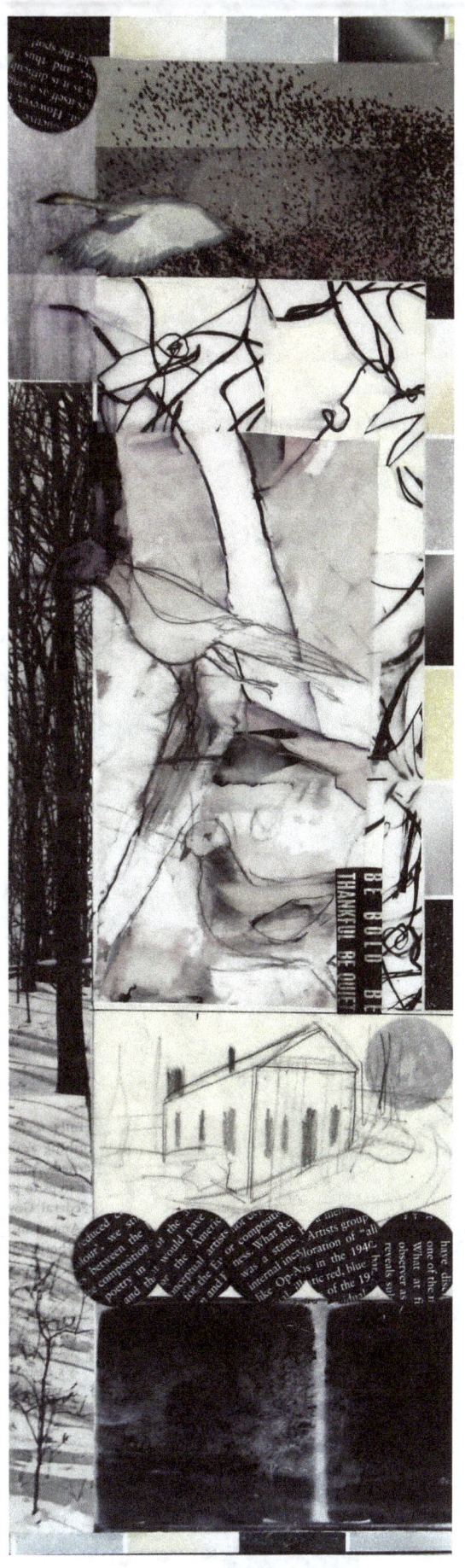

Be Bold, Be Thankful Be Quiet
Encaustic wax collage on wood panel
5" × 16" (13cm × 41cm)

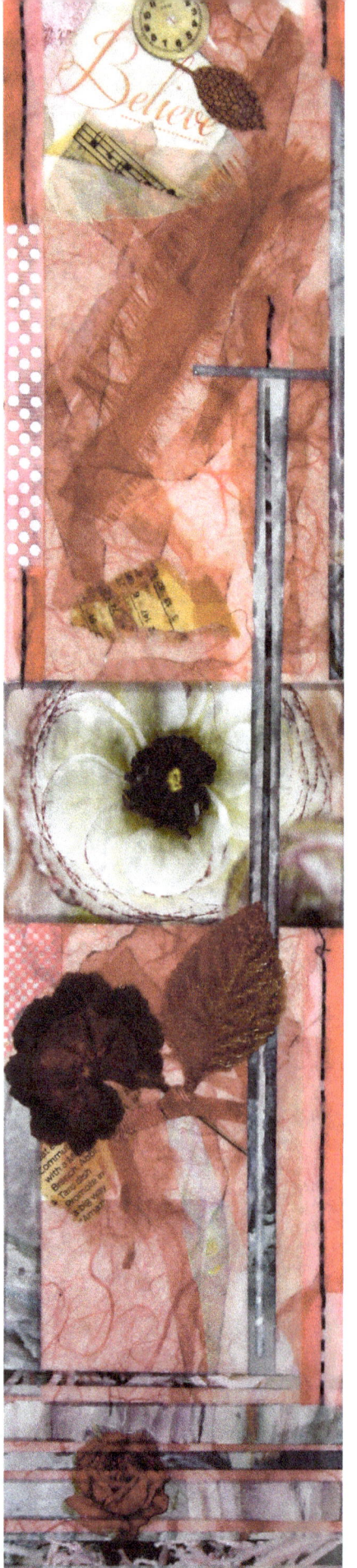

Believe
Encaustic wax collage on wood panel
3½" × 15½" (9cm × 39cm)

I would never have paused to ask myself design questions during the creation process before my Hollins art education. I either liked a piece of art or I did not. My professors at Hollins taught me to put my personal bias aside and ask a lot of questions which I feel keeps an artist moving in a forward direction.

The following are a few more "back off" questions I have culled from my art journals from the years I was enrolled: Where is the movement? Does it keep me involved and on the canvas? Are there simple surface forms or are there more complicated things going on? What are the representative forms trying to say to the viewer? Are there perspectives, if so, where do they lead? Do they lead off the canvas or stay within it? What mood does the color convey? Is there a message in that? Are there any symbols, if so what are they suggesting? Where are the intersections and convergences and how do they work within the whole? Are there areas of calm, if so what is the effect? It is stagnant (negative) or it working in a positive way? Where are the areas of energy? Are they working to hold my interest? Where are the negative spaces?

In Professor Michael Gettings' Philosophy of Art class he announced the first day that if we were there for answers we would be disappointed because philosophy was the art of asking questions. He was right, as asking questions is an art in itself.

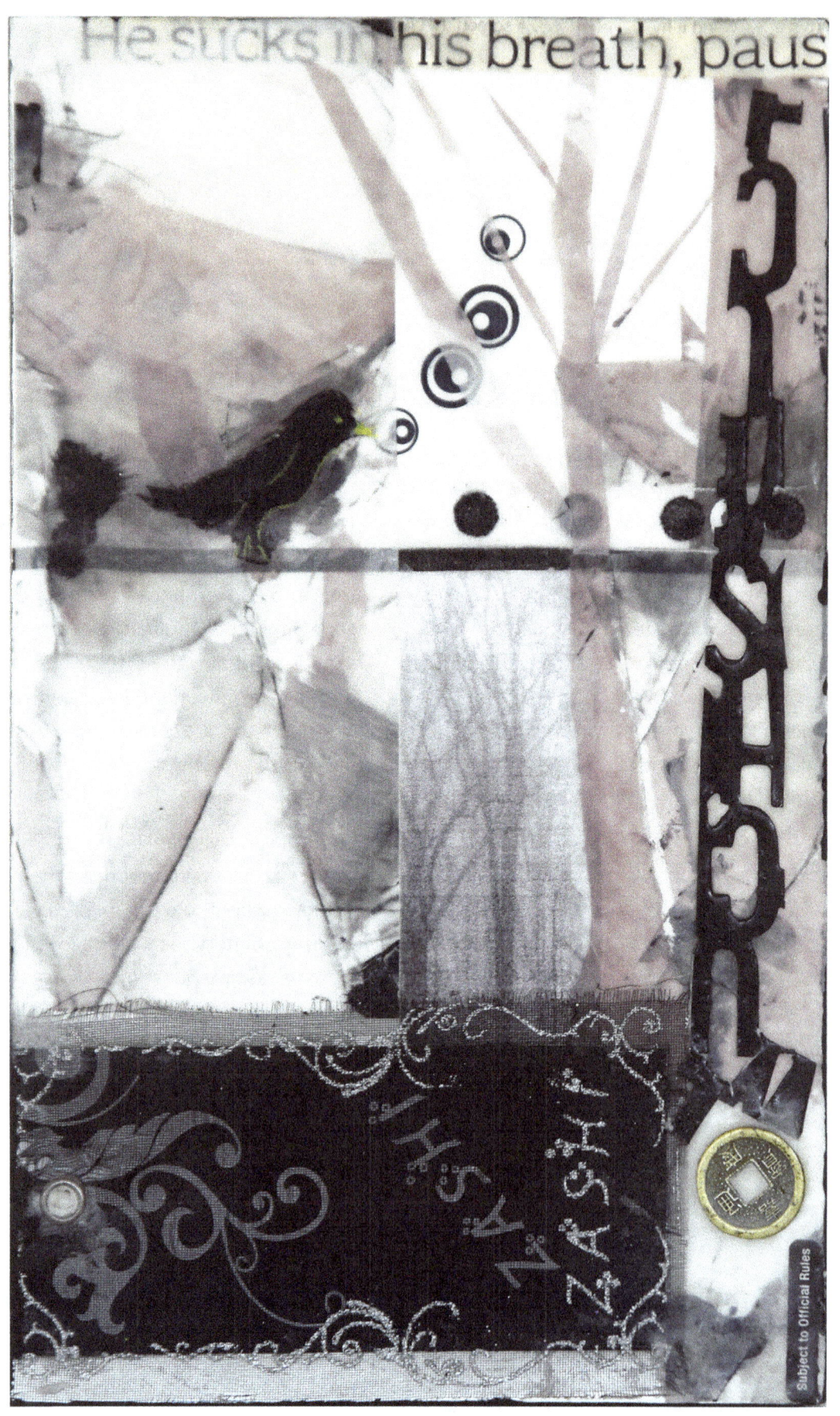

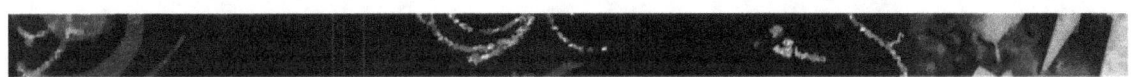

I have spent a great deal of time trying to figure out what it was about the work that so obviously spoke to the buyers of my first show. This is what I have decided about that body of work as well as the rest of the pieces in this book. I feel this work is working on two levels.

First, there is just enough visual information through images of the natural world that the viewer can get some sense of a narrative. Although it is not my intention, these forms and images bring a certain amount of comfort and contentment to the average non-artist viewer. Birds, cages, trees, horizon line or sky are some of the images that work as representational. When working, I am always asking myself what is the least amount of information I can express and still get the idea across to the viewer?

Second, once the viewer is pulled into the art with recognizable images, the viewer begins to examine the subtleties of symbols and re-cycled items that make up the abstract backgrounds and are held there. I would hope that this also means I am going in the right direction with good art design principles!

Backgrounds in my work include items found in daily life such as clothing tags, bits of lottery tickets, Japanese stock market pages, etc. They are mostly recognizable but they are used in an abstract way for color, pattern, or shapes. This second level, I feel, is what makes the work interesting and holds the viewer's attention. It is driven by my desire to re-cycle. I call my style "barely representational into abstraction."

The show I had at Hollins with my last independent study work sold quickly and was astonishing to Professor Dahlstrom (and myself). She assured me that it was very rare for an artist to sell all of a body of work, especially a new artist.

Blackbird Sucks in His Breath
Encaustic wax collage on wood panel
5" × 8" (13cm × 20cm)

DETAILS IN THE LAYERS

I hope this section inspires you with new ideas of how to reuse materials in your art work that would end up in the trash, as well as inspiring you to delve into the magical world of encaustic wax art.

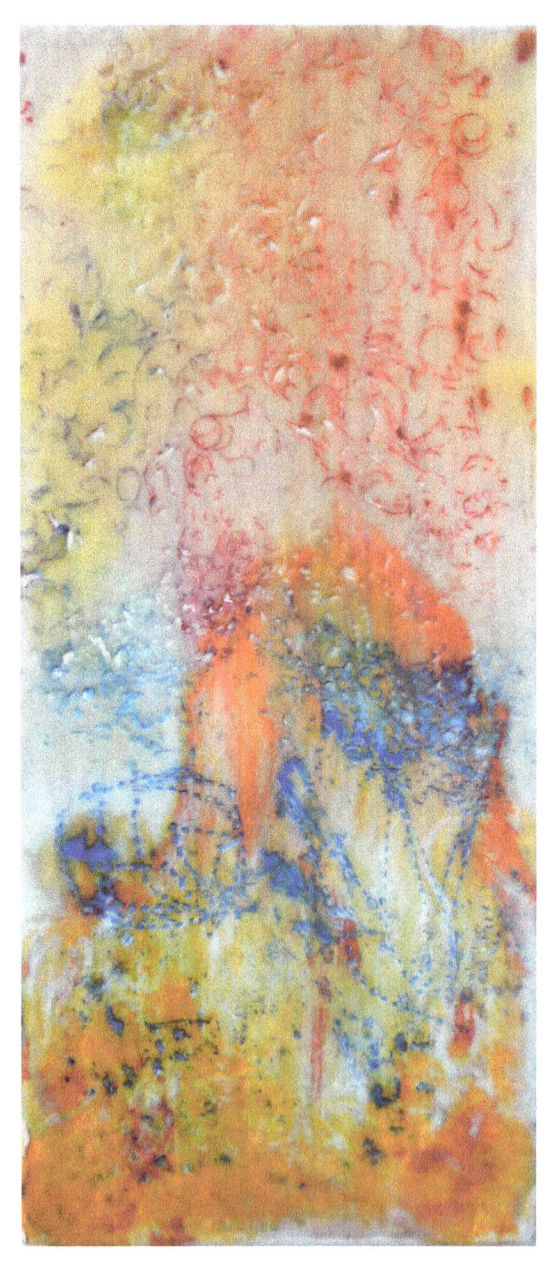

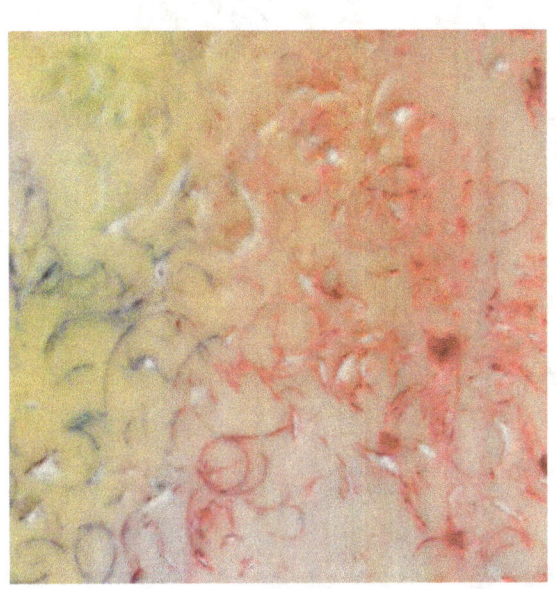 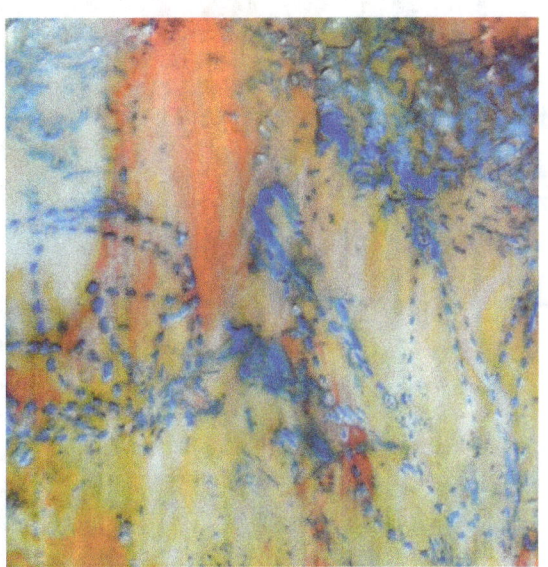

Incising — Pot Scrubber

In the top half of this piece, the circular lines are made with a kitchen metal pot scrubber. Oil wax stick—blue on the left; red on the right—was rubbed over the texture and filled the indentations. Canola oil on a paper towel, wiped off the excess, leaving the marks made by the scrubber filled with color. You can see I chose to leave some of the pink staining on the surface around the red circles.

Incising — Sewing Tool

This texture was created with a metal sewing pattern transfer tool. It leaves dash-like lines. I chose a blue oil paint stick to fill in the lines. This sewing tool can be used to draw with and reminds me very much of using an etching tool on a copper plate that has a resist applied to the surface. (Also used for art on page 126.)

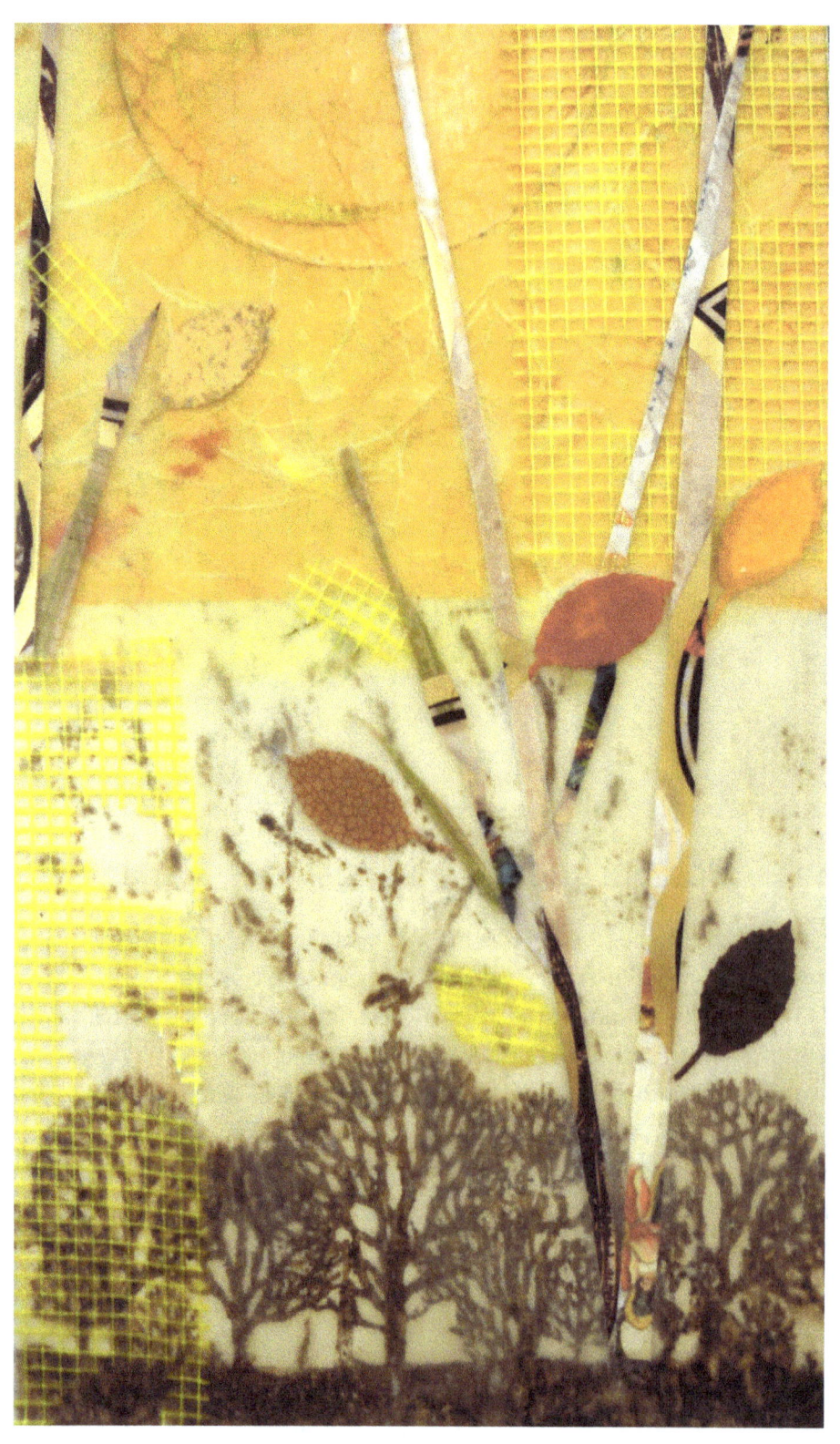

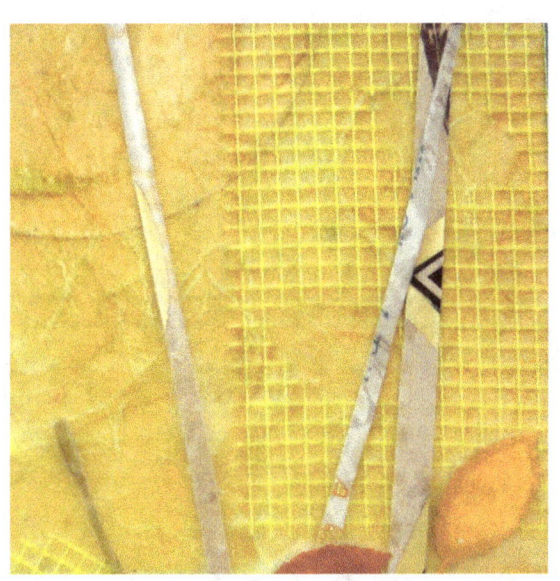

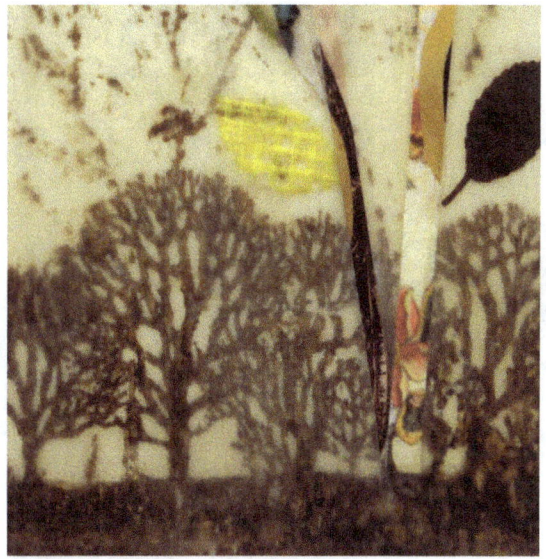

Drywall Tape

Yellow gridded tape— used for drywall seams—on the top right and lower left is also repeated in several leaf shapes. My intent was to use it as a stencil, build up the wax in a squares pattern and then lift when the wax cooled, but I actually liked it as a design element and decided to leave it alone. It was applied in the last coat of clear wax medium. I then sealed the entire piece with a coat of clear medium and fused.

Image Transfer

A transfer using a toner-based photocopy of a stand of trees. (Transfer method described in detail on page 88).

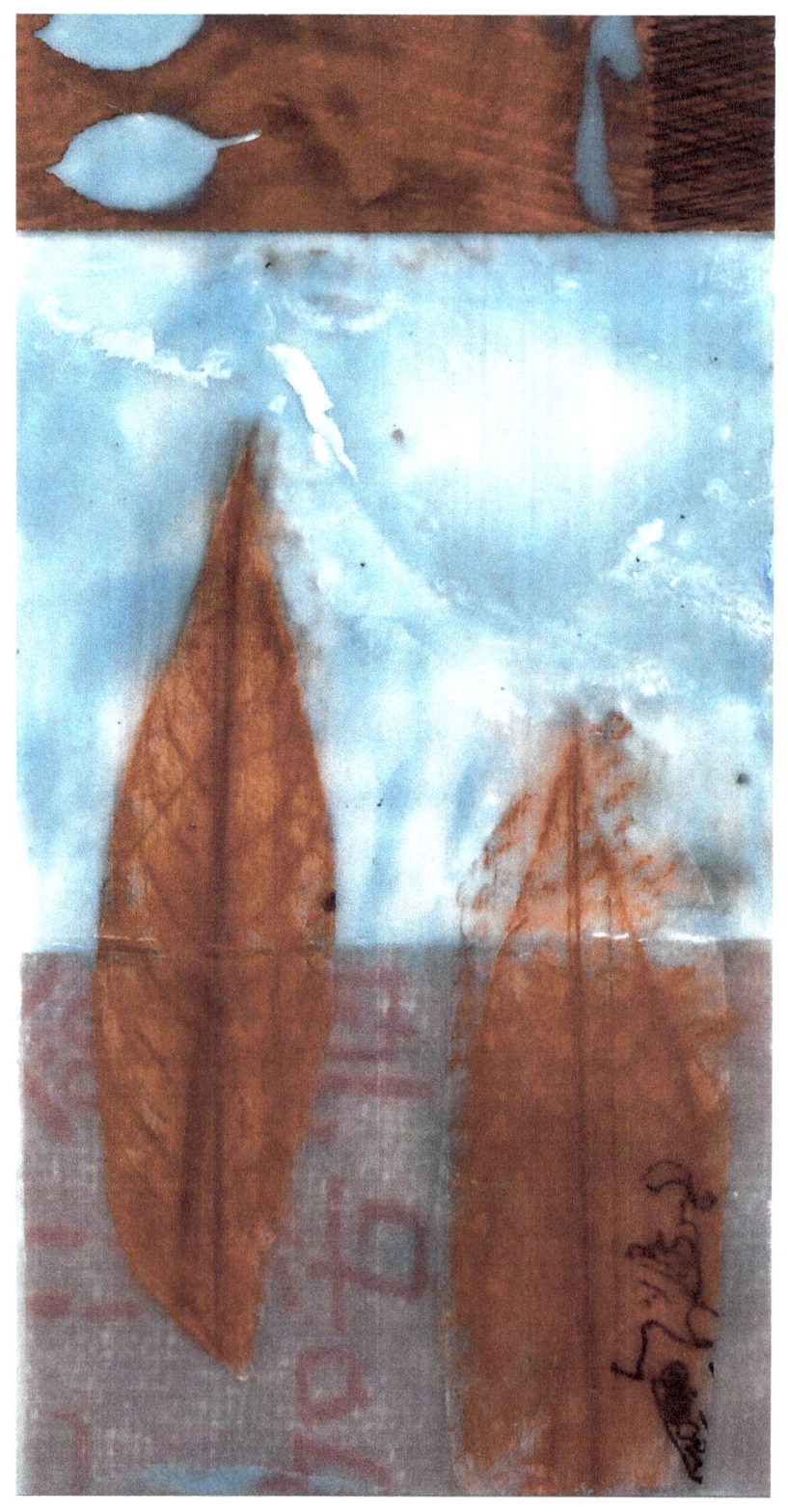

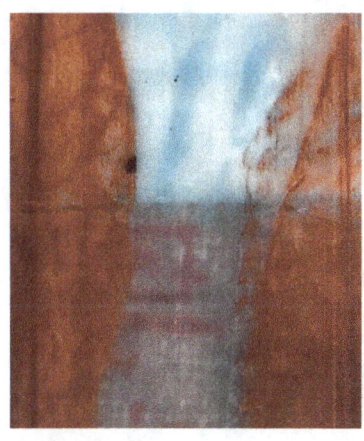 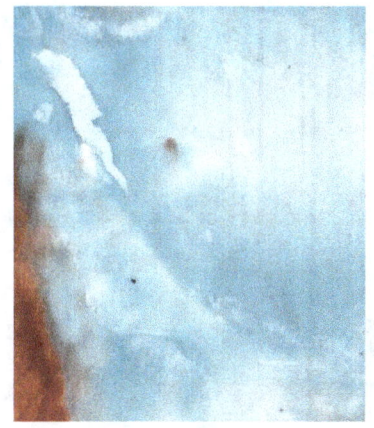 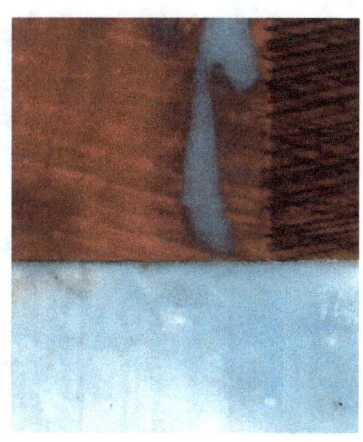

Layered Paper

Japanese writing paper is embedded in several layers of clear wax. Closer to the surface, are two leaf rubbings on tracing paper. I have cut close to the edges of the leaf so the paper nearly disappears. After laying down one layer of clear wax medium over the tracings, I scribbled on the surface with a fine black permanent marker (bottom right) mimicking the Japanese text. I then added one coat of clear wax medium and fused for a final coat.

Modeled Wax

The center blue area is an example of modeling the wax. One layer of light blue pigmented wax went down first, then a layer of opaque white pigmented wax. After it cooled slightly, I used a razor blade at an angle and scrapped off a lot of the white, letting blue show through. Above and to the right of the left leaf is a blob of pure opaque white. This happens if you do not clean off the razor blade regularly as the wax builds up on it. White was re-deposited onto the surface in a different place. I chose to leave it alone as I liked how it looked.

Merging Designs

The top portion has a background of wallpaper with two punched-out leaves. The first layer of blue background shows through the leaves. The mottled clear wax medium distorts the pattern of the wallpaper but shows clearly to the far right where I used very little wax medium. The wallpaper design has lines drawn on it. I dribbled some blue pigmented wax on top of the wallpaper to continue the color onto the right side of the art piece as well as a bit at the bottom.

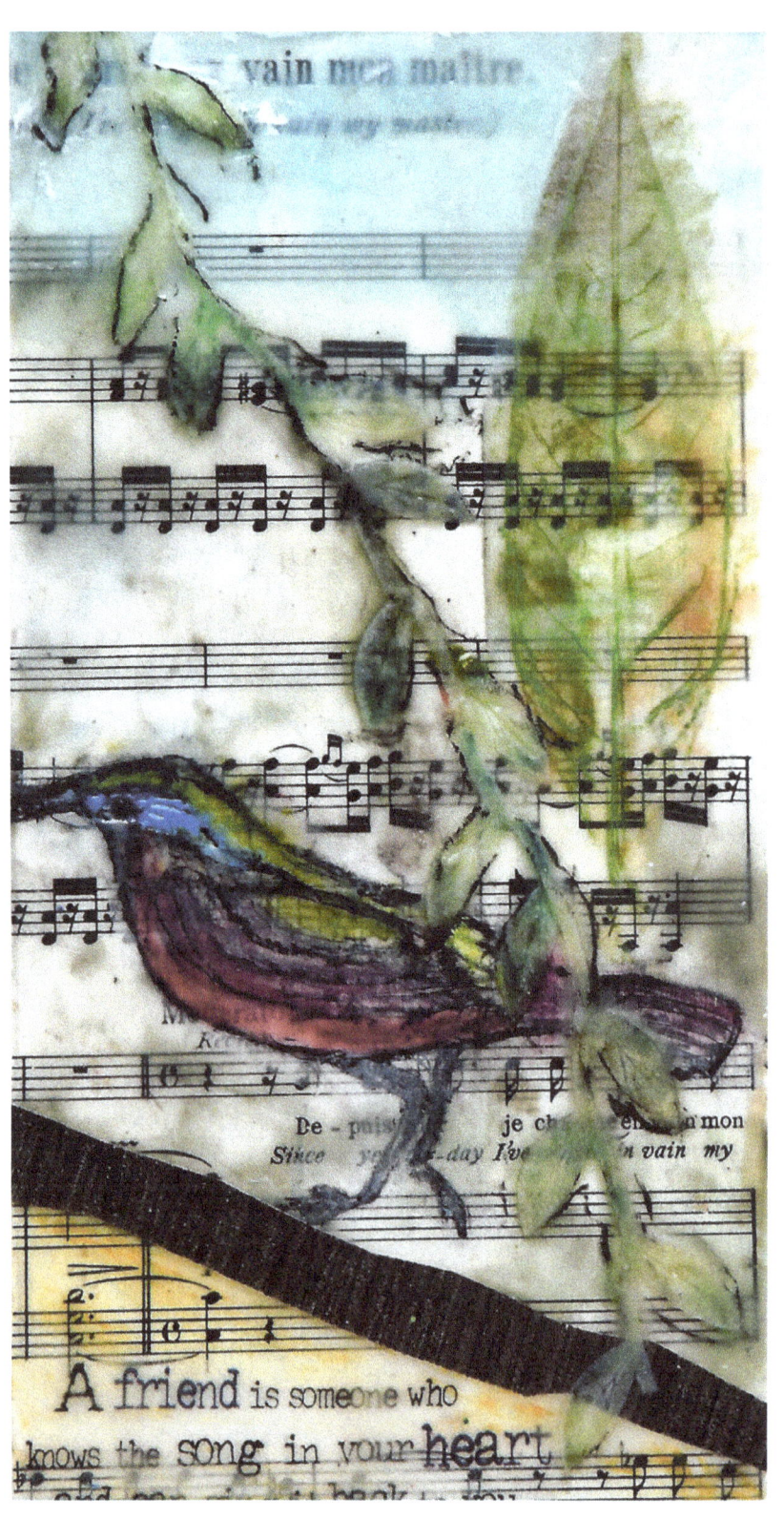

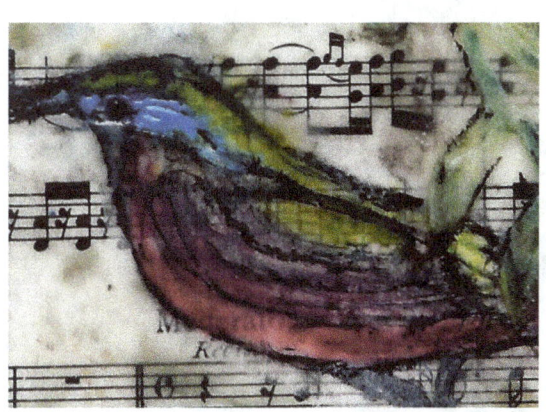 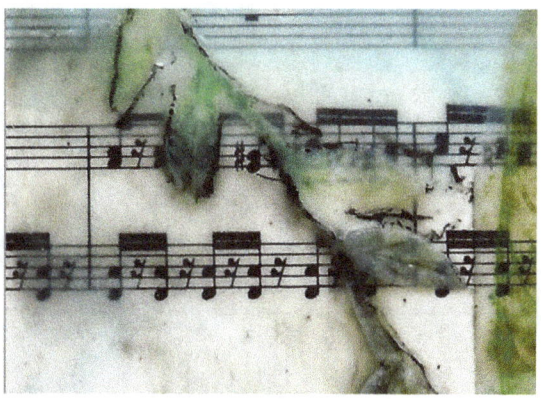

Embellished Transfer

Antique sheet music glued to the substrate forms a background and hand-cut textured wallpaper makes a branch for the bird. The bird was then transfered to the surface. I used small brushes to paint colored wax in yellow, red, and blue onto various parts of the bird. At this point, I can still see the transfer underneath.

  I applied one coat of clear wax medium and fused. With a sharp tool, I incised the outline of the bird and filled in the grooves with black oil paint stick. I cleaned the surface with canola oil and paper towels, added one layer of clear wax medium and lightly fused.

Decorative Ribbon

The top right side has a leaf rubbing on tracing paper in green and orange. The branch of leaves running diagonally down the work is a specialty ribbon that I dipped in translucent green wax and applied to a warm wax surface, pressing in with my fingers for good adhesion. I then painted some of the leaves with a fine brush and a darker green pigmented wax. Next, I used clear wax medium to coat the entire piece and fused. As I did with the bird, I used a fine sharp tool and outlined the leaves and filled in with black oil wax sticks, cleaning the surface with canola oil. One last clear coat of wax medium was the final step and one final fusing.

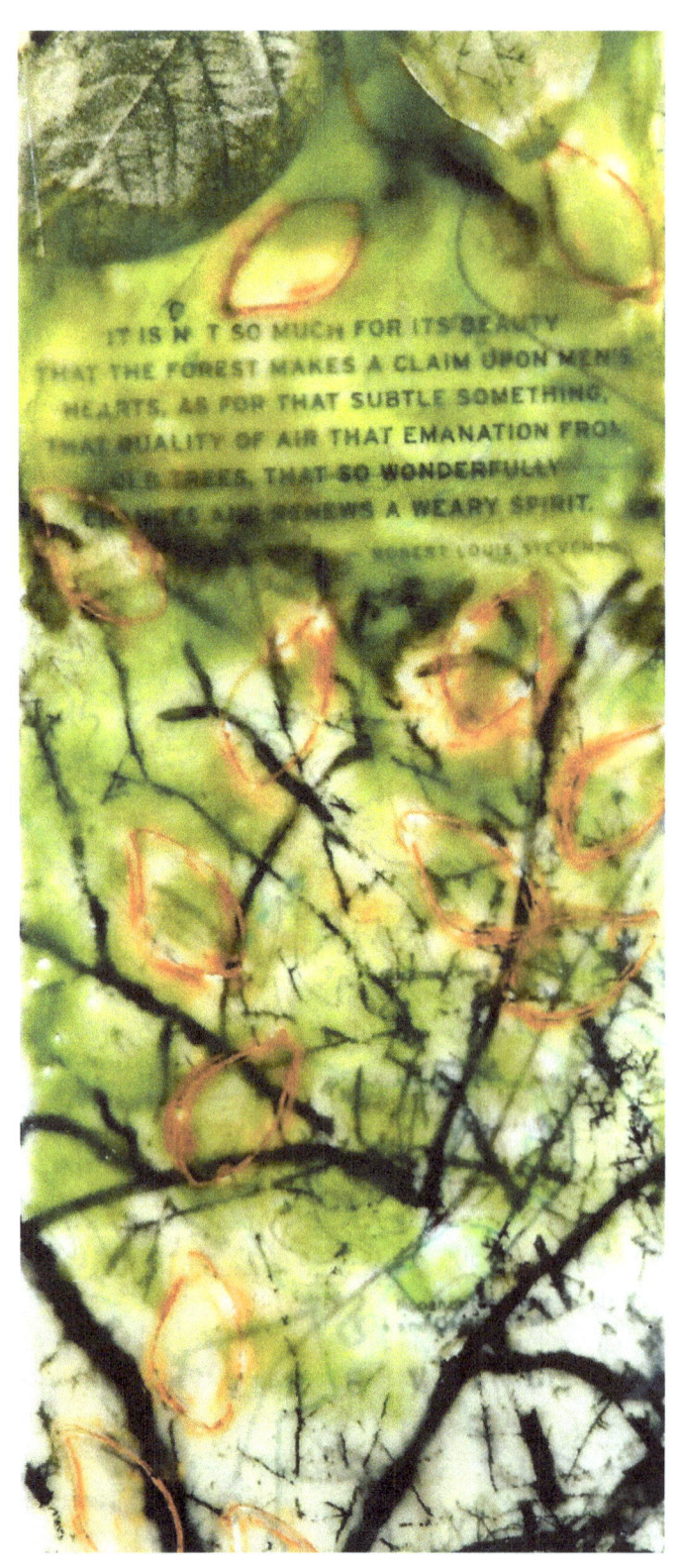

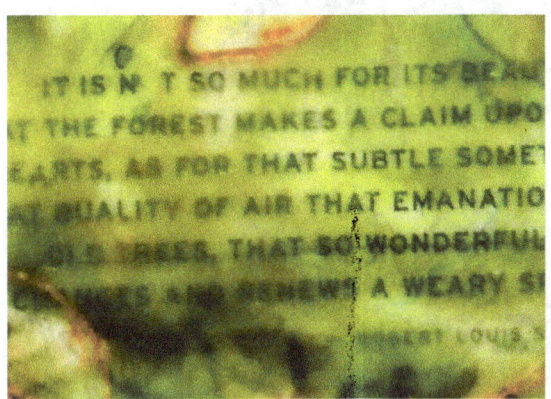 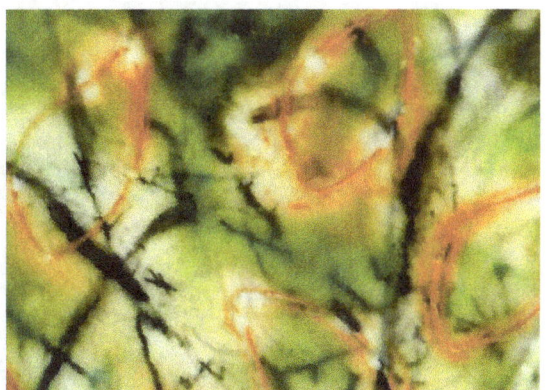

Mirrored Image Transfer

This is a small section of a much larger piece. The two leaves at the top is a section of wallpaper that I hand-cut out and glued to the substrate. The Stephenson quote is a transfer and, as you can see, applied slightly off-kilter which I did for interest. The copy of the quote was done using the mirror image function on the copier machine. The second layer is a translucent green and yellow pigmented wax painted onto the surfaces with brushes and fused. The next step was a transfer of complex tree branches using a black and white photocopied image, then a clear coat of wax medium and fusing.

Cookie-Cutter Incising

A small leaf cookie cutter made the incised leaf pattern which I then filled with an orange oil paint stick. I then cleaned the surface with canola oil, added another clear coat of wax medium and fused. One last clear coat of wax medium and fusing finished the piece. Note the subtle peeking through of the underlying map.

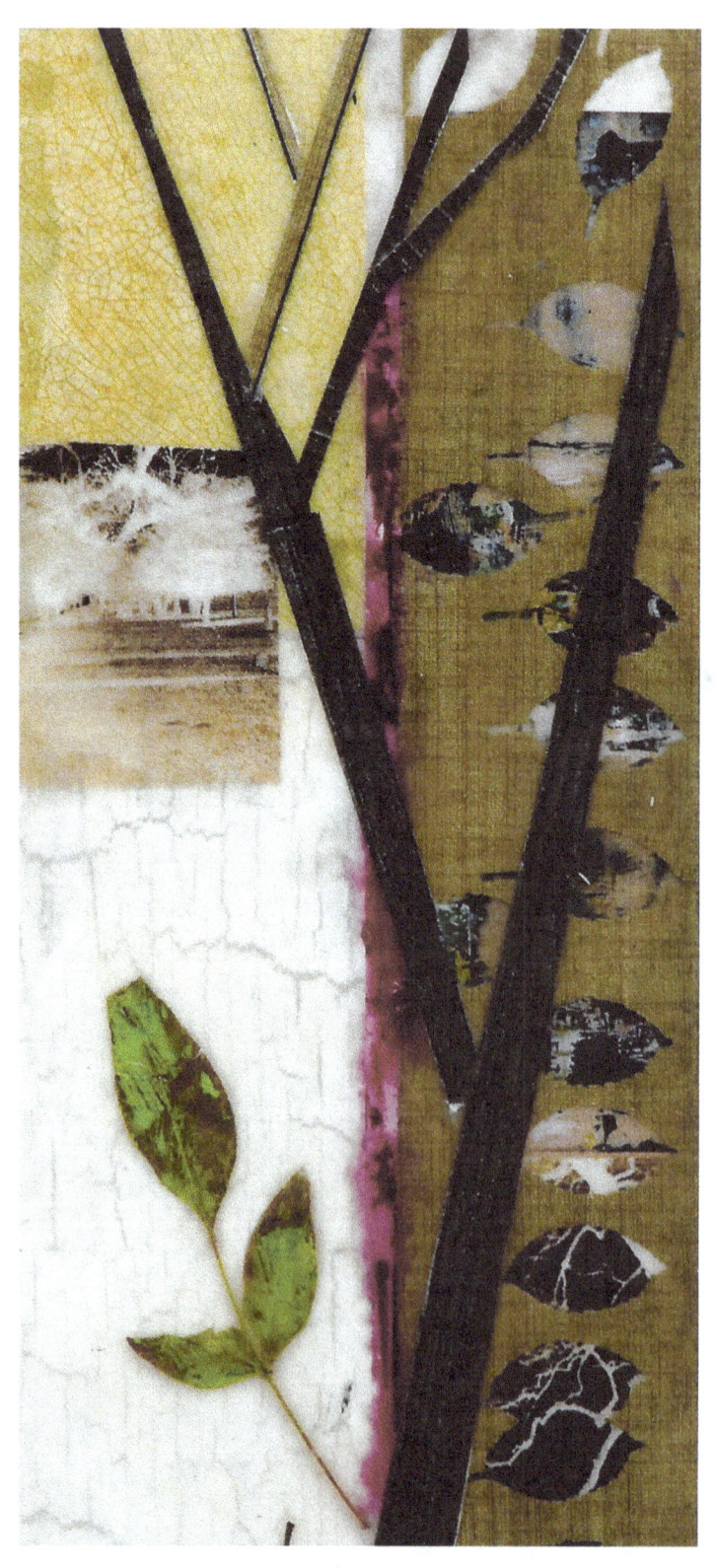

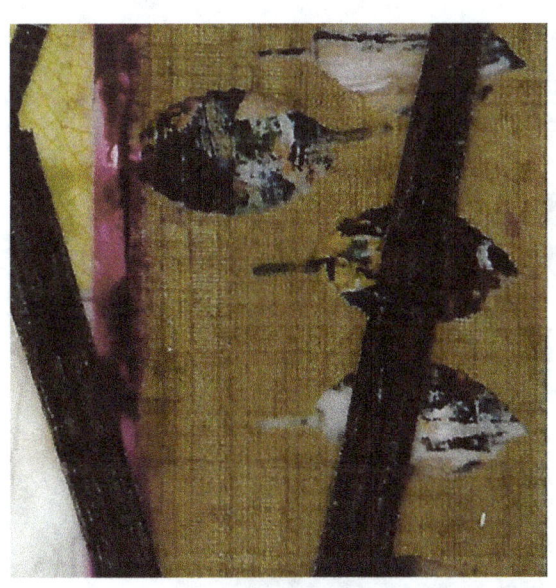 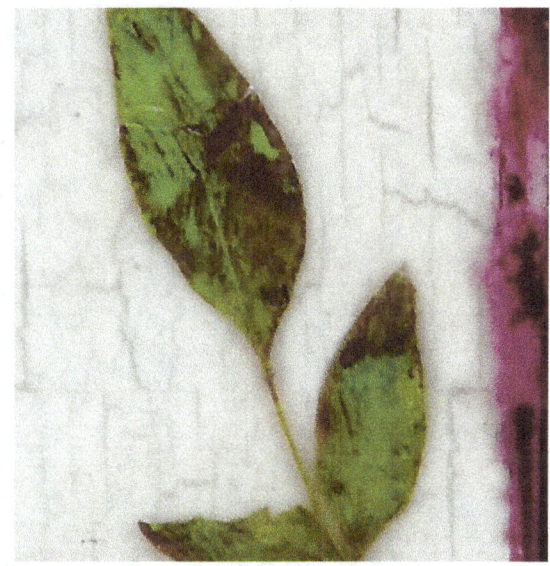

Punched Shapes

A favorite technique of mine: incorporating the positive and negative images of punch-outs. In this case, it is a strip of wallpaper on the right hand side of the piece that is the negative to the punched-out pieces that are scattered elsewhere in the piece. I have backed the negative with very interesting marbleized paper, gluing them to the back and letting dry completely before gluing them to the substrate.

Natural Materials

The left bottom has a white paint chip sample glued to the substrate and a real dried leaf glued to the paint chip. Dried natural materials can be used if pressed and thoroughly dried. The slightly off-center fuchsia line that bifurcates the piece is pigmented wax painted on with a fine brush. There is only one coat of clear wax medium over the surface of this piece which is fused at the very end.

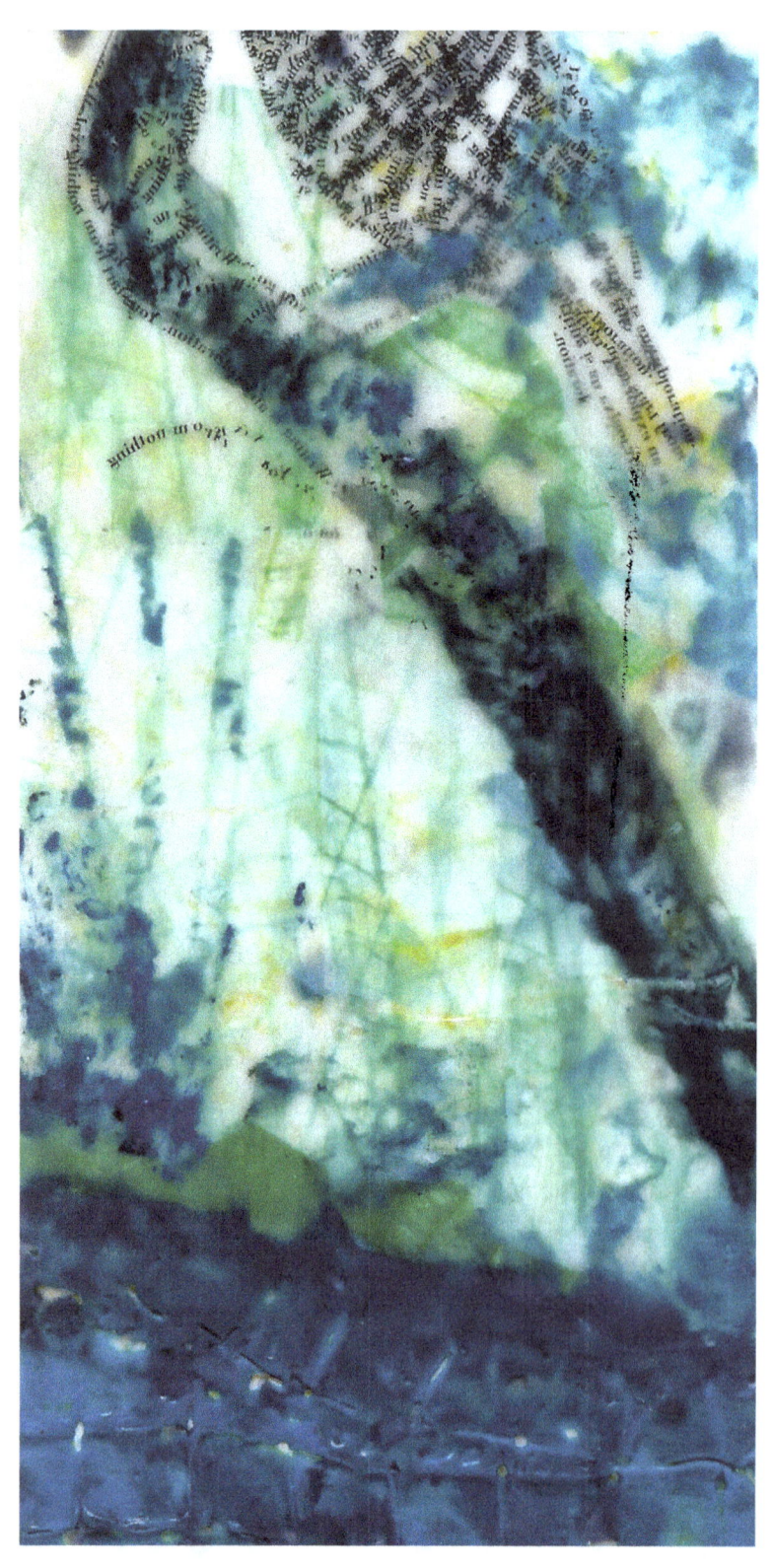

Sheer Color

Sheer blue and sheer green wax—created by mixing a generous amount of clear medium with pigmented wax—were dripped and painted onto a white background, leaving areas of white.

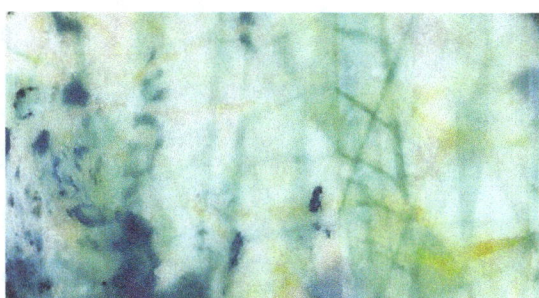

Cellophane

Cellophane Kleenex wrappers (travel size) with a delicate veined leaf pattern were used as a layer. (Cellophane curls if the heat gun gets it too hot, so apply a generous amount of wax first, and then fuse very carefully.)

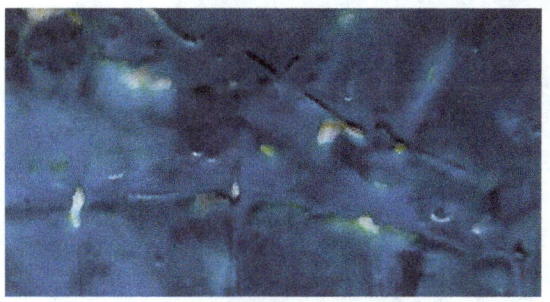

Opaque Build-Up

The bottom was stenciled with a piece of ½" (13mm) square grid fencing material. I ran the flat hake brush over the surface many times to build up the wax which gave the blue an opaque quality with a lot of density. I let the surface wax cool slightly and then lifted the metal "stencil" up carefully, leaving a gridded pattern in the wax.

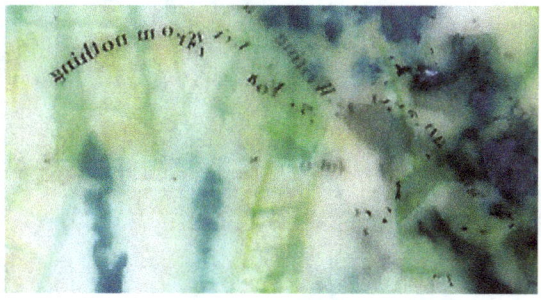

Drifted Transfer

At the top of the piece, is an image of a bird made with text. It is a transfer that was made with a copy of a magazine advertisement. I intentionally did not use the mirror transfer so the words are not readable. Note that the words have drifted away from part of the bird. This happened when I over-fused and the wax became liquid and drifted. It was an accident but because I loved the result, now I often do it on purpose.

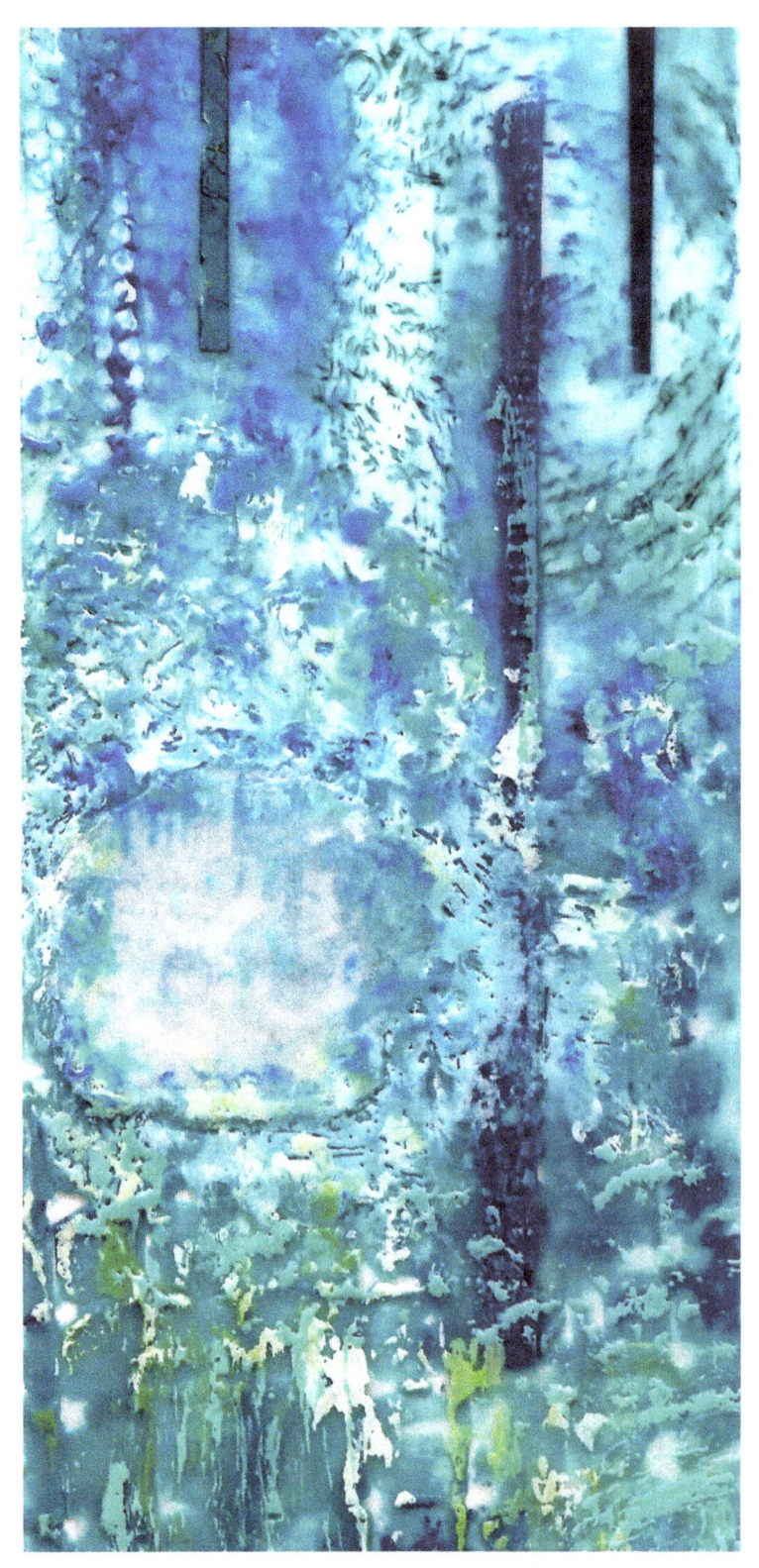

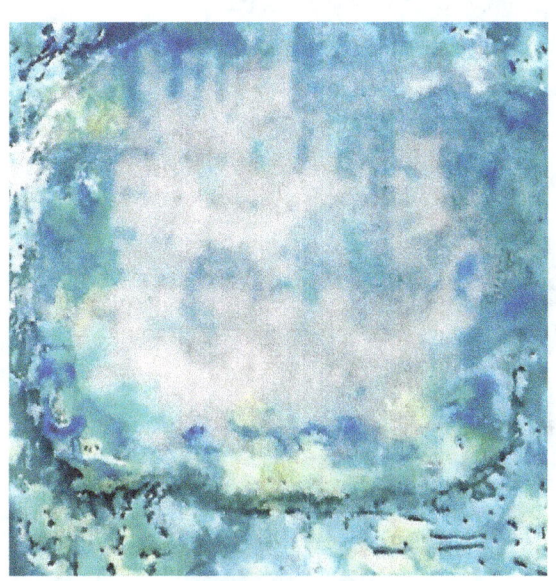

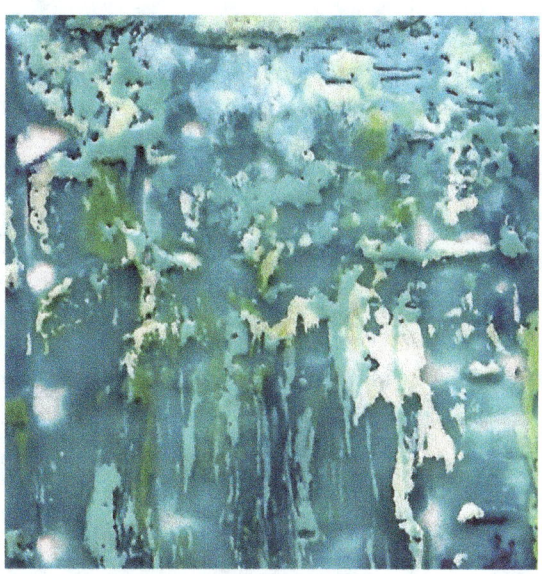

Personal Photos

A solar plate print of me and my baby sister sitting in slatted lawn chairs with me hovering over her protectively. I named this piece "Drowning in Memories."

Texture Build-Up

This piece has a watery feel. The bottom is a great example of scraping with a razor blade to get interesting patterns and also of letting wax cool slightly on a flat brush and running the flat side sideways over the high spots, leaving bits of color. This builds up texture in a piece.

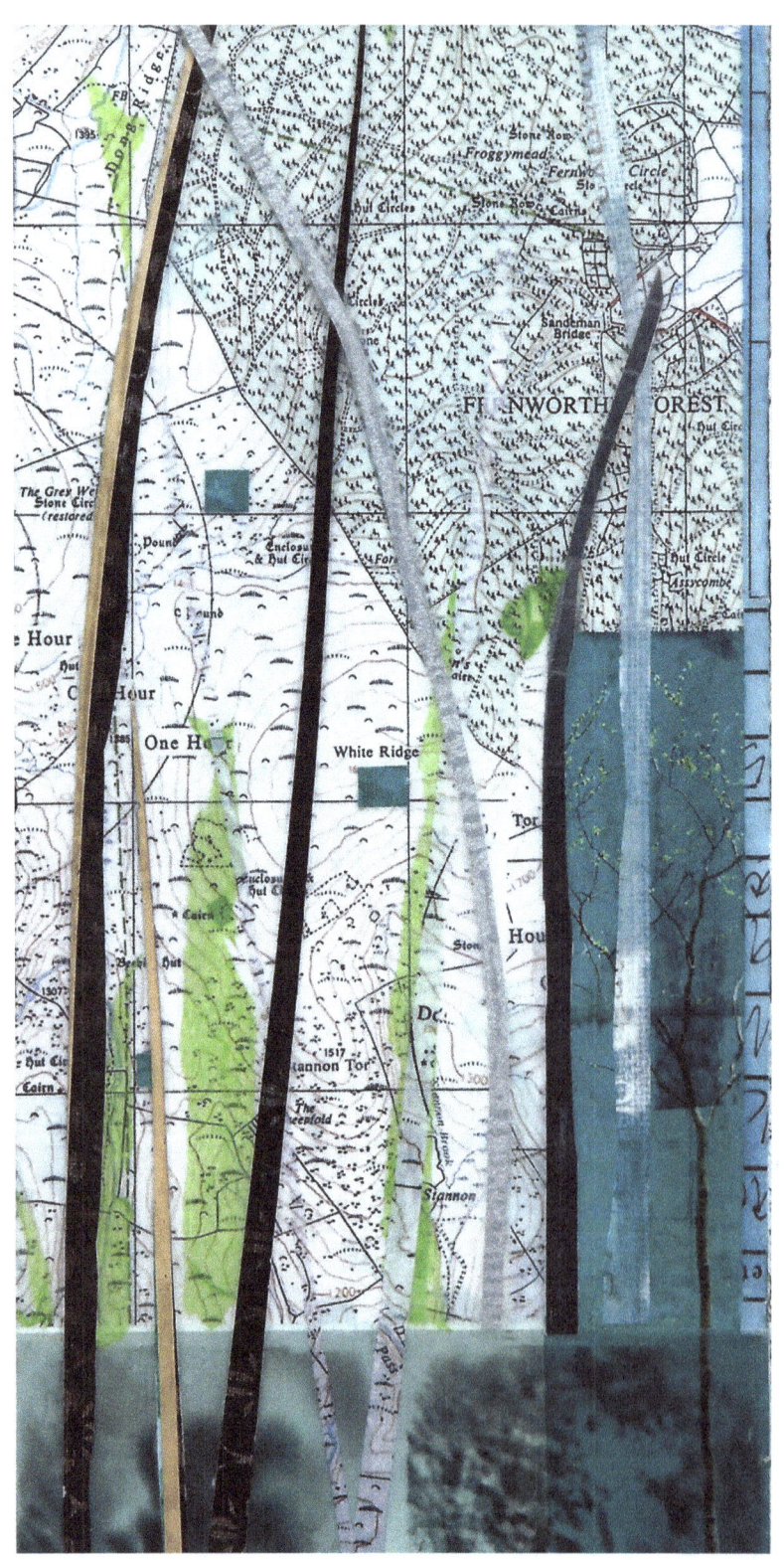

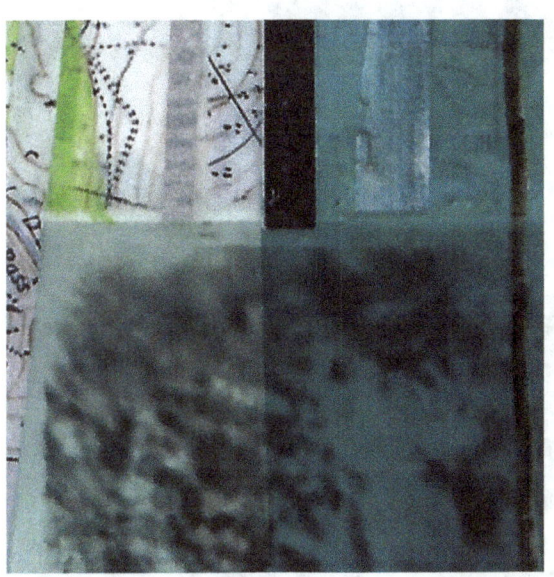
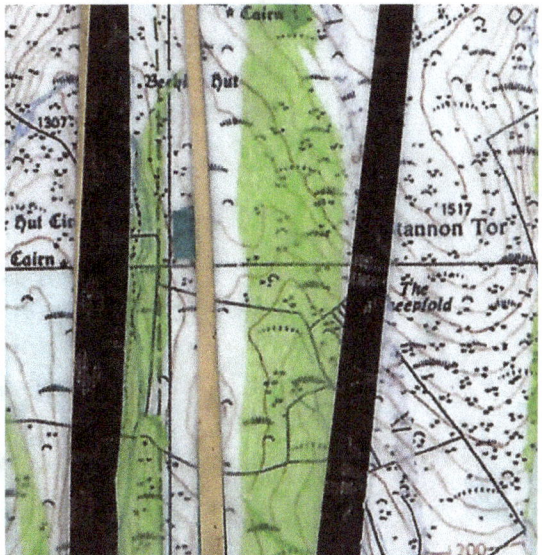

Film Negatives

A strip of photo film negatives at the bottom with indiscernible images in them creates a haunting quality.

Tissue Paper

I have used lime-green and light-blue tissue paper to carry the eye around the piece and add layering. This piece has one coat of clear wax medium on top.

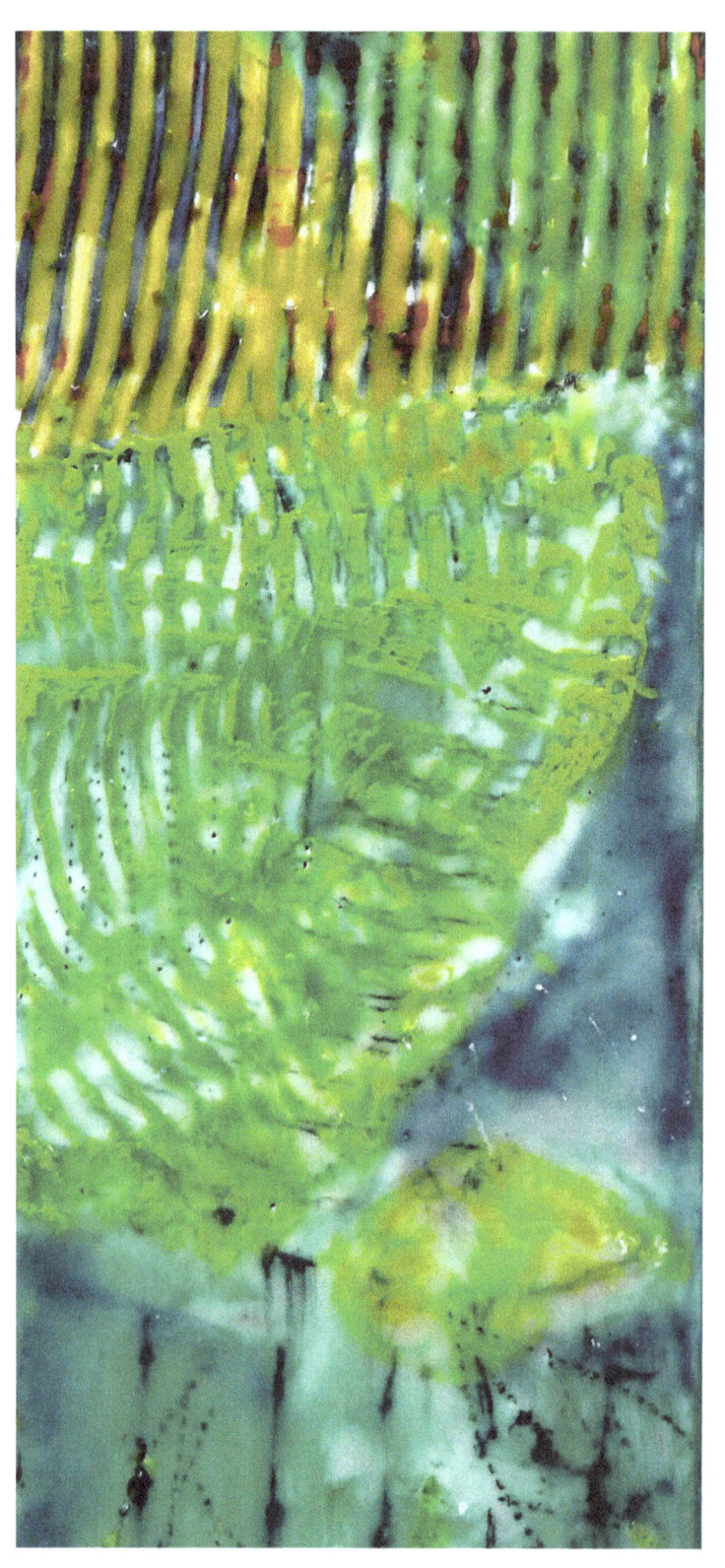

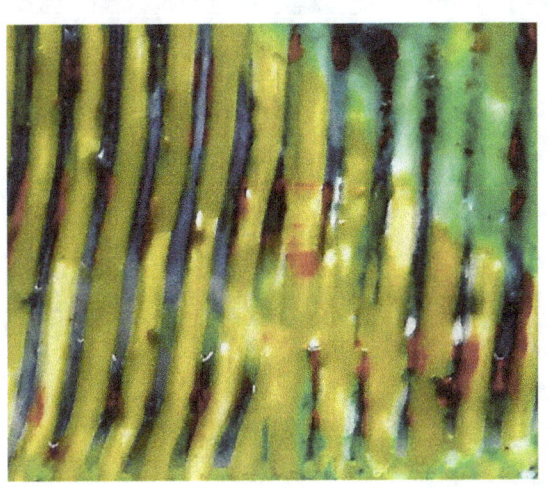

Re-Melting Wax

An example of a piece gone wrong and salvaged. In the top of this piece things were happening I did not like, so I re-melted it and while the wax was still warm I plunged a carved wooden batik stamp in the shape of a textured leaf into the soft wax. It gave me the sharp ridges that I then ran the flat side of a brush against in red, yellow and dark blue.

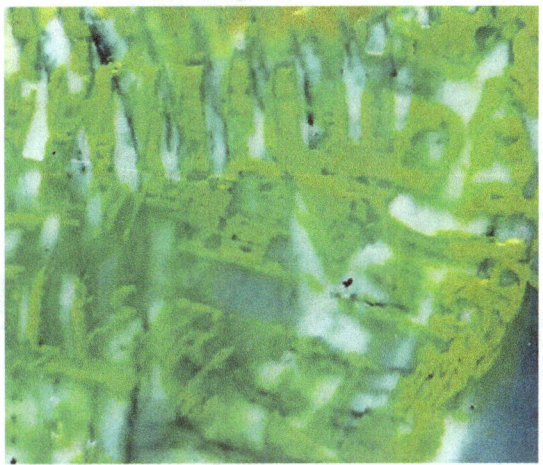

Oil Stick on Raised Areas

The leaf in the middle was more to my liking. It has been a modeled blue-and-white background. I then used my metal sewing roulette wheel over the top and filled in with a dark blue oil paint stick, cleaned with canola oil and added one coat of clear medium to the surface and fused. Again, while the wax was warm, I plunged the batik leaf stamp into the wax, leaving ridges. This time I used a bright green oil stick to run over the ridges, then one last coat of clear wax medium and fused lightly.

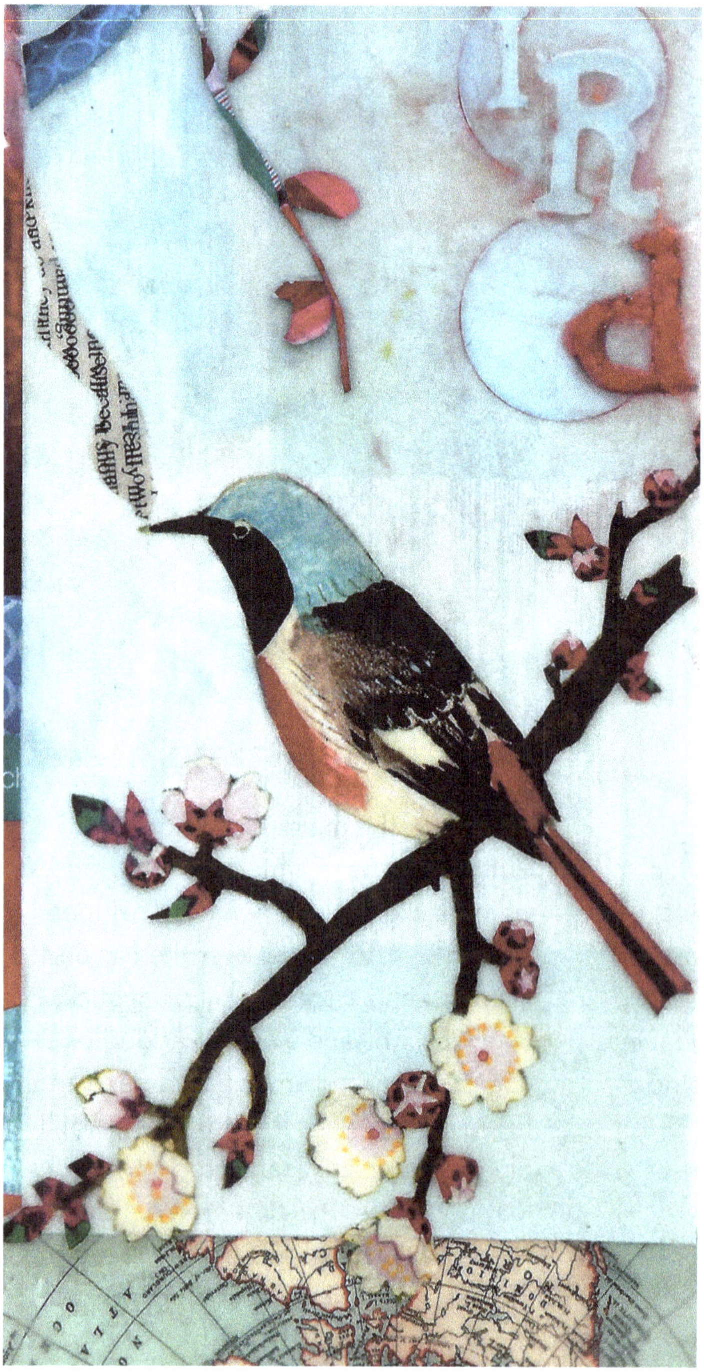

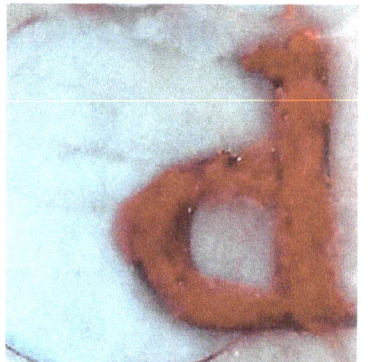

Stickers

The I, R and D letters and the circles beneath them are stickers. To unify them, I applied red oil paint stick to the surface and then wiped it off leaving the red around the edges.

Collaged Paper

Magazine strips and wrapping paper bits were used to compose this hand-cut tree branch and bird.

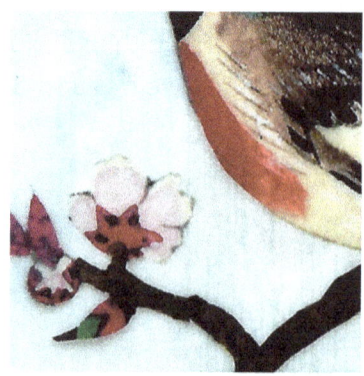

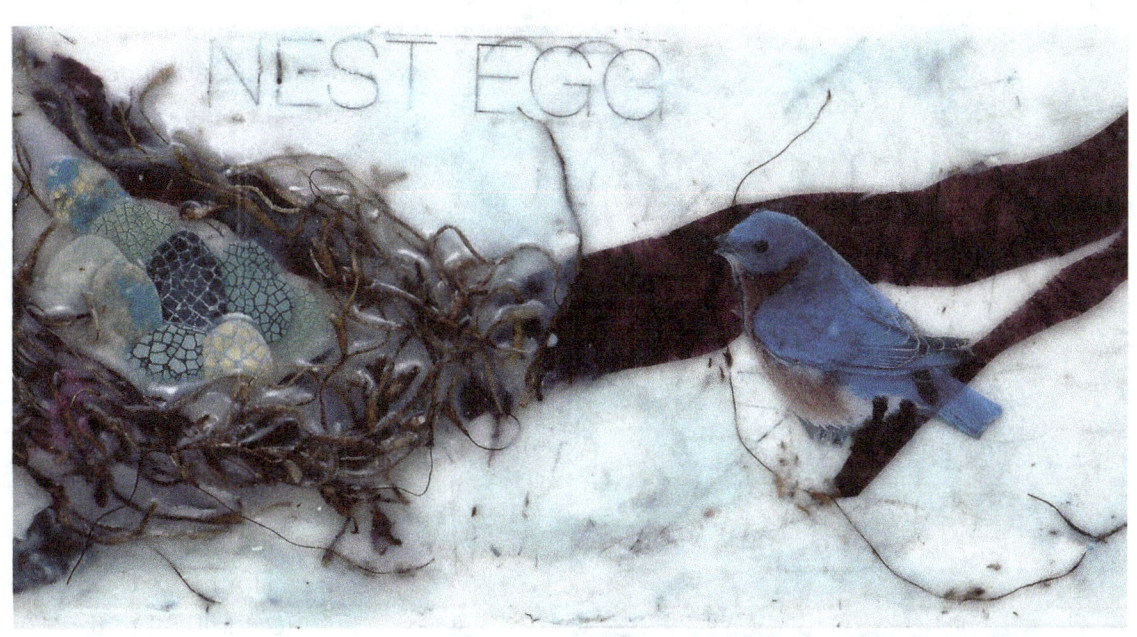

Dimensional Objects

The nest was made of sphagnum peat moss. You can clearly see the thickness of wax used that is holding it in place.

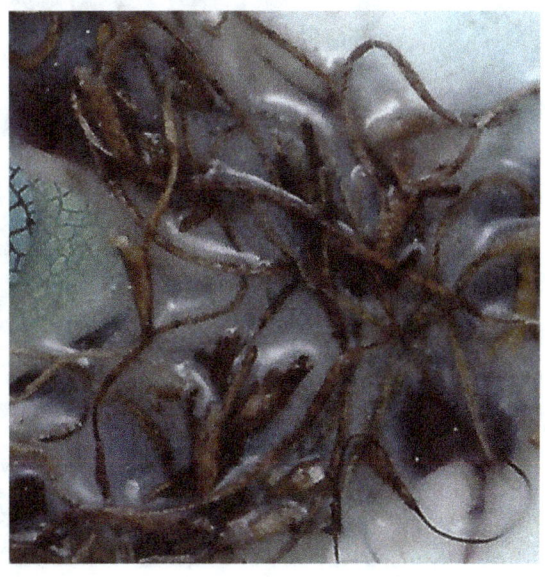

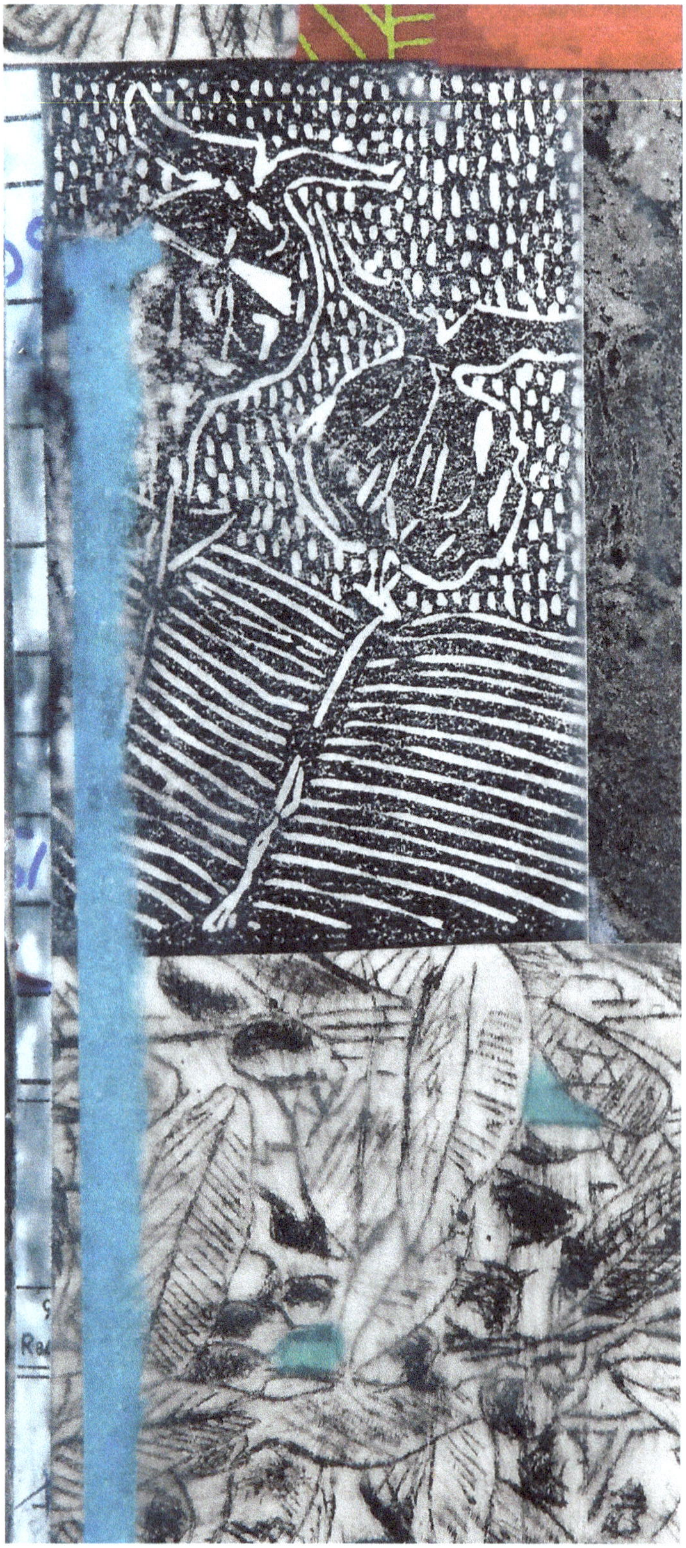

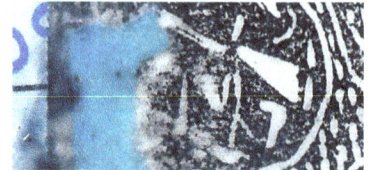

Clever Repair

A detail of one of my first pieces of encaustic wax collage. I used a linoleum-cut print of a poppy seed head that tore slightly in the printing process. The tear is strategically covered by the blue piece of handmade paper to the left side.

Newsprint

A rescued-from-the-trash piece of blank newspaper worked for me to draw on prior to adding it to the bottom of this piece. The far left side is shredded paper from the trashcan. One coat of clear fused on the surface.

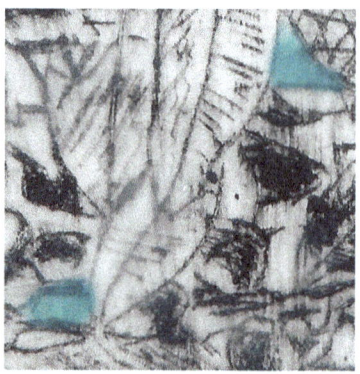

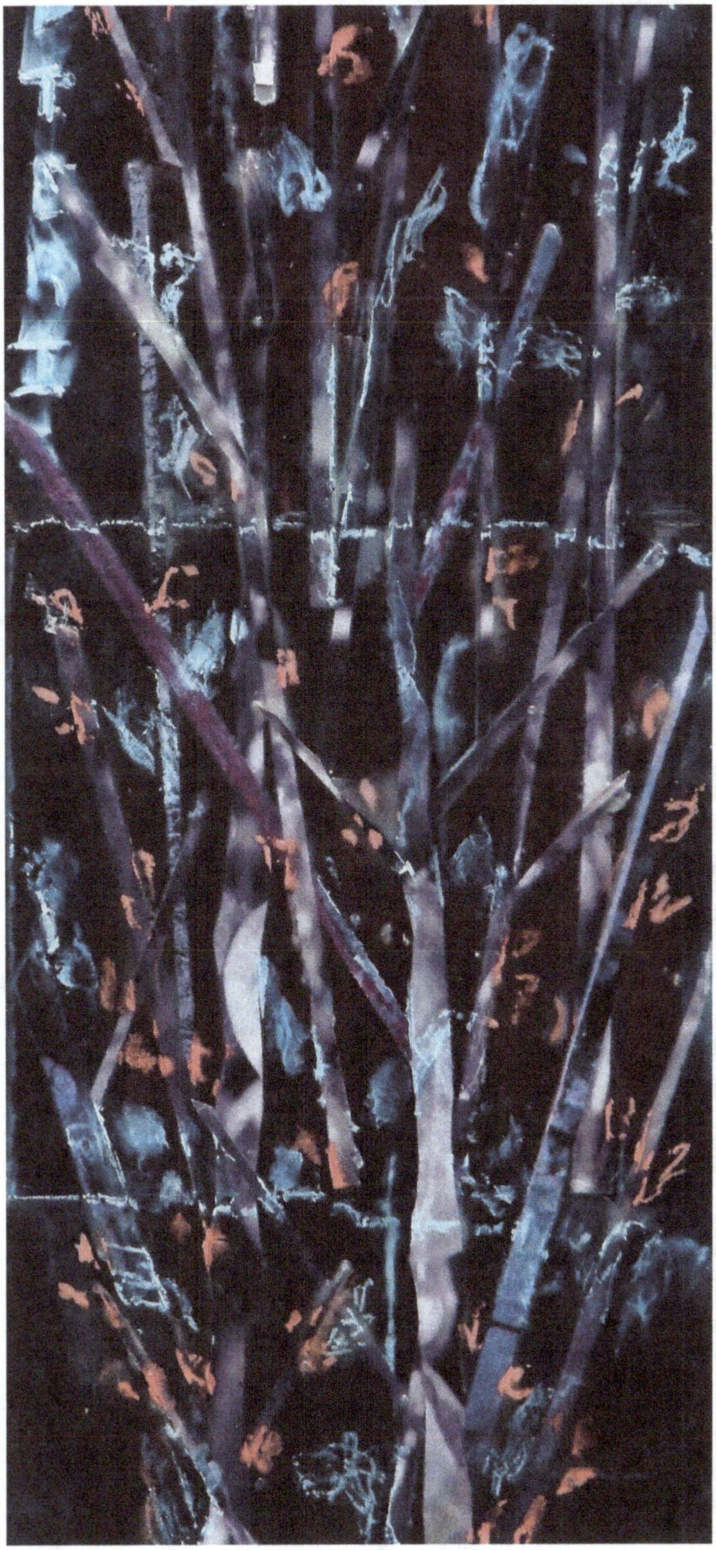

Metal Shavings

Copper shavings from sanding the edges of copper plates are embedded here in the wax. Additionally, tired belt sander sheets with subtle patterns left from the sanding of copper etching plates makes up the background in this piece though it does not convey well in the photograph. There is only one coat of clear wax medium over the surface.

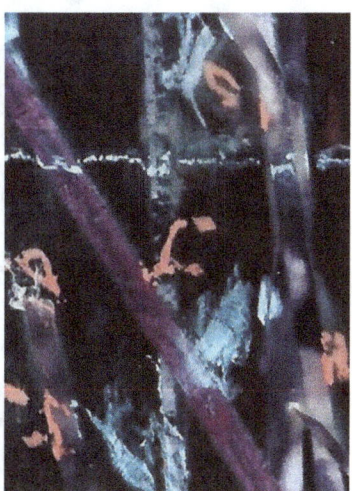

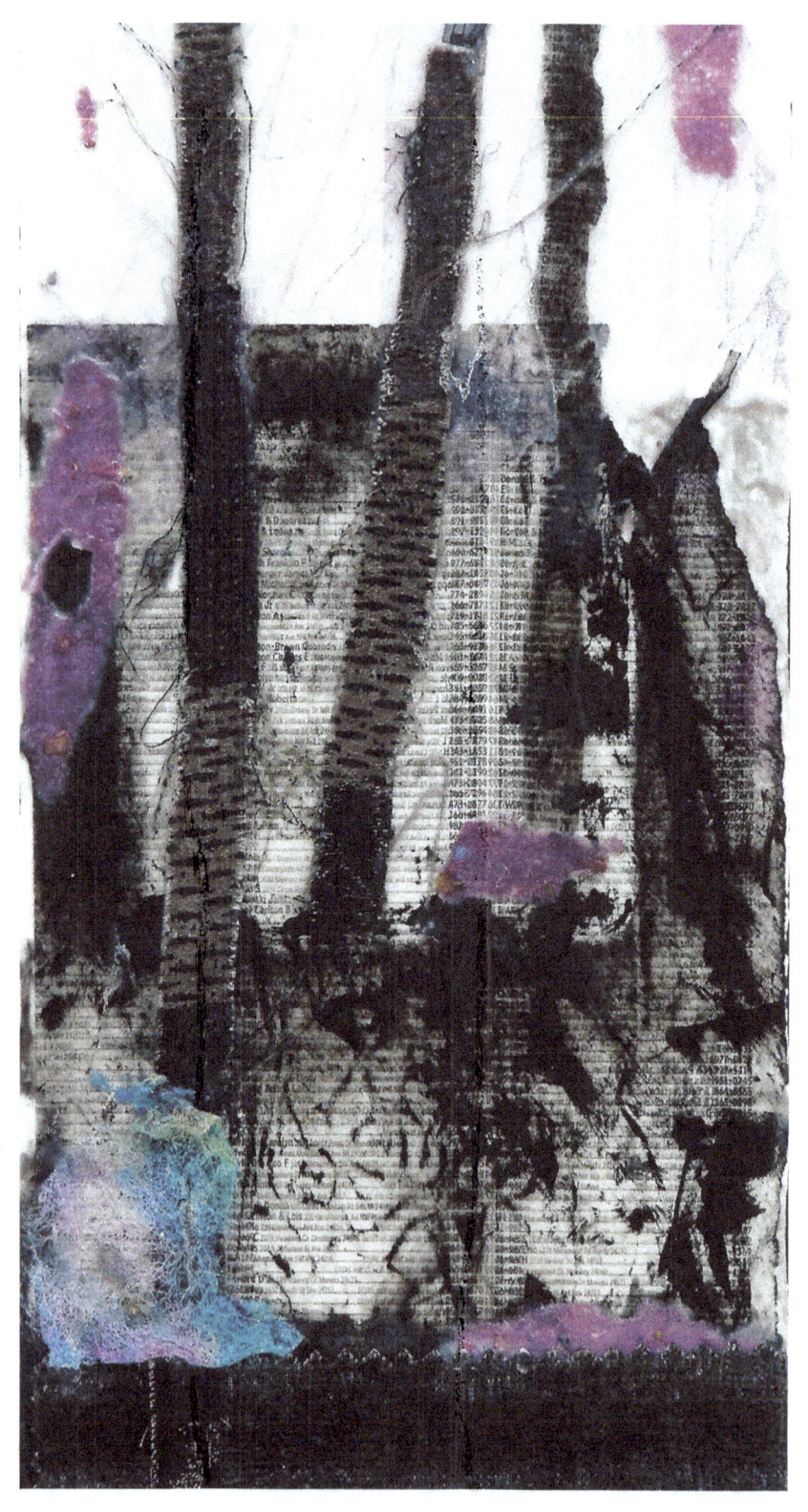

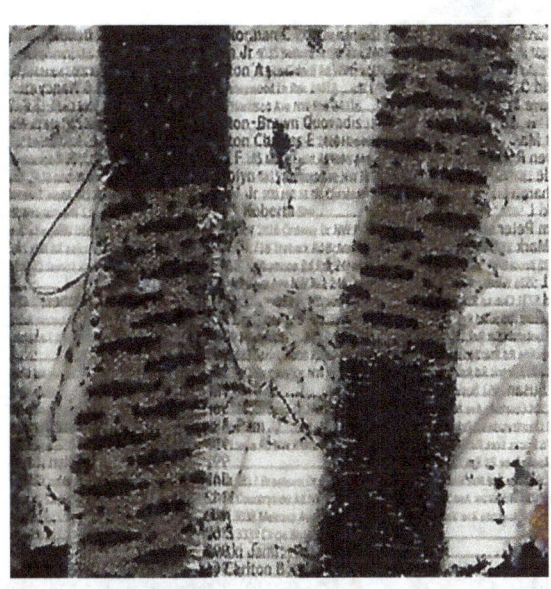

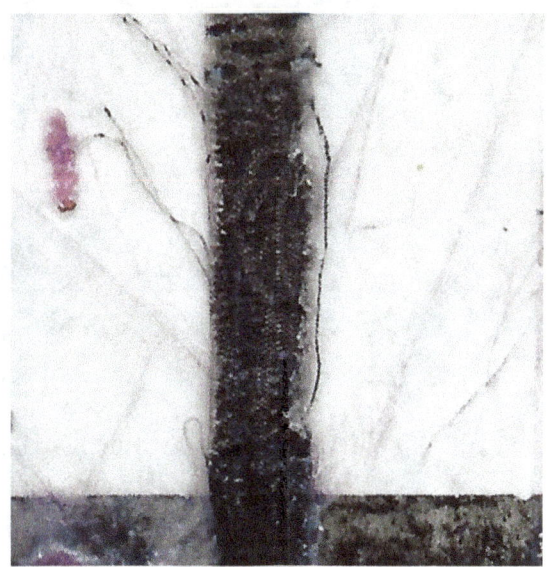

Heavily-Textured Fabric

Textured upholstery fabric at the bottom has very little wax on it so as to see the detail of the fabric texture. The two center trees are made from leftover strips of fabric from a dress my husband made for me.

Industrial Paper Products

The background at the top is industrial roll paper towels in which I used to clean off the brayer after a day of etching. The towel would catch in the brayer, folding and wrinkling the towel, leaving a heavier ink mark that looks a lot like a forest of trees and saplings in winter to me. I used the paper napkins in many pieces of work.

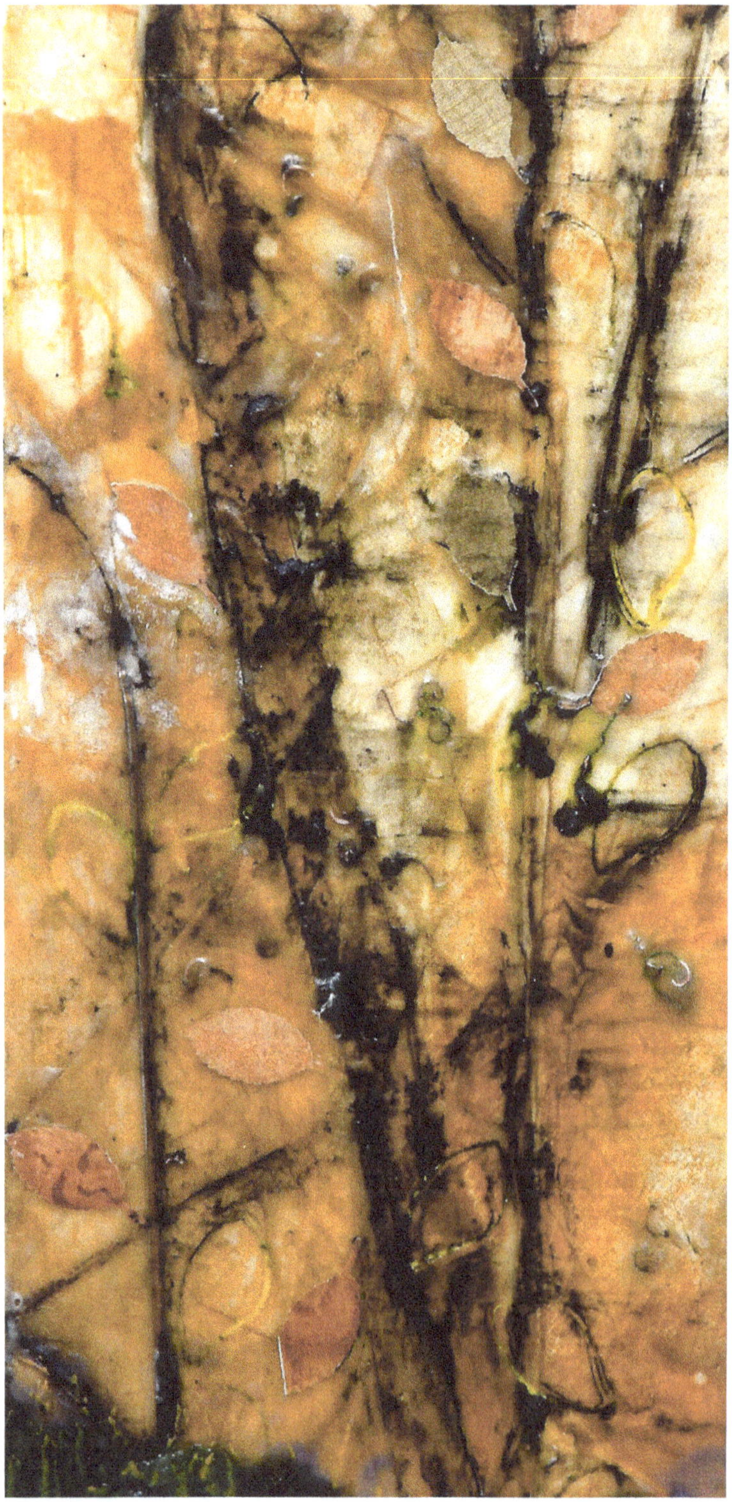

Wax Crayon

The trees are drawn with black wax crayon, hitting and missing some areas.

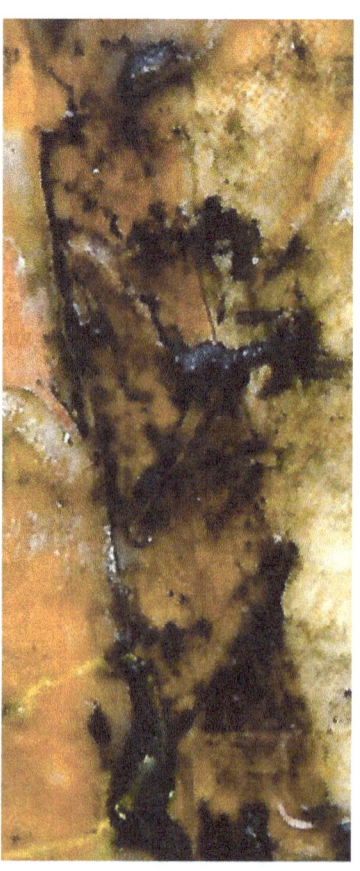

Ghost Marks

The bottom clear circle that plays off the black paper cutout above, was made by using a piece of paper cut into a circle, then dipped into clear wax medium and pressed into a warm wax surface, then lifted. It left some wax which is what you are seeing. The result was this delicious ghost-like mark that reminds me of ghost prints in monotype.

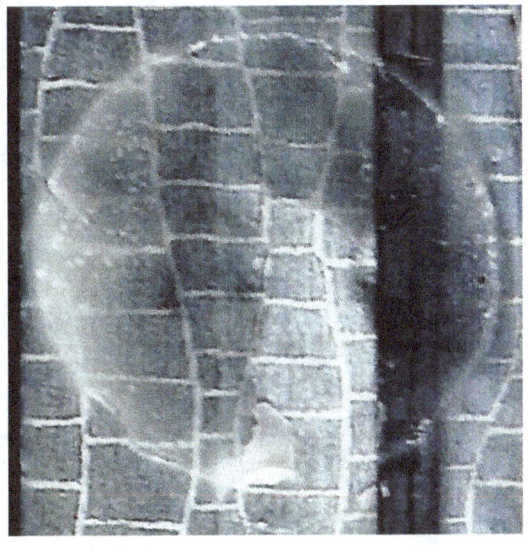

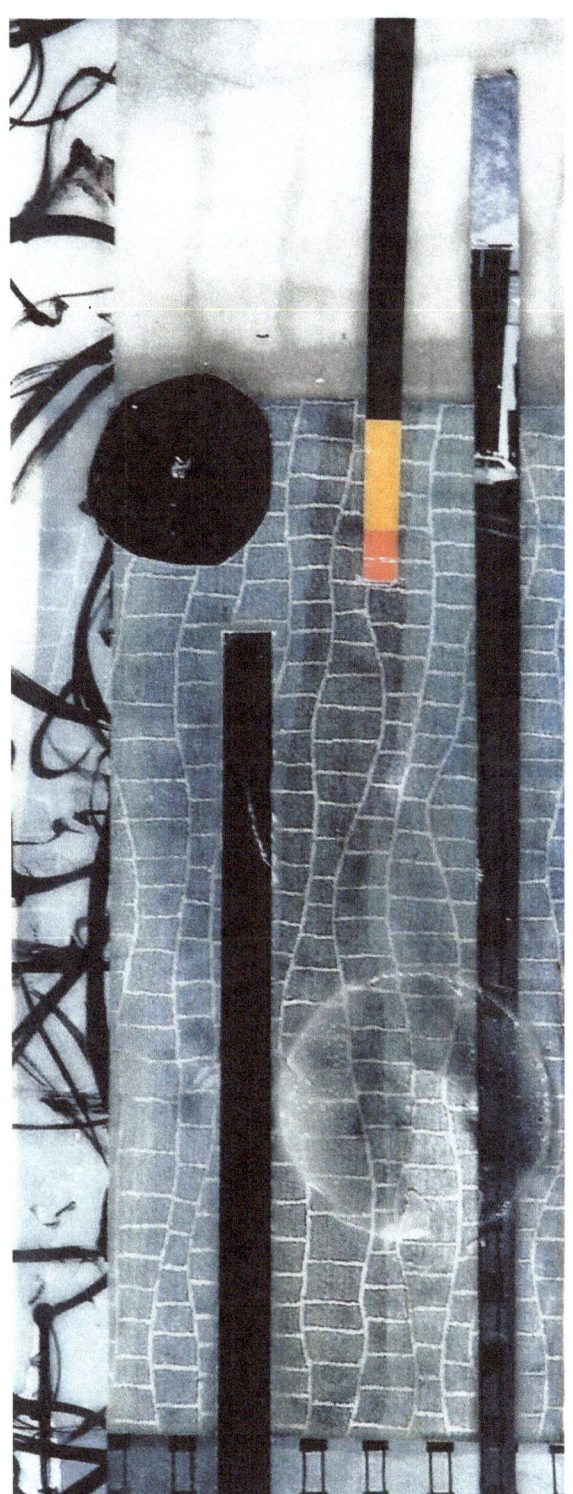

EXTRA LAYERS

The pieces in this final section repeat many of the techniques explained in the previous section, but I wanted to include them to provide even further inspiration and allow you to see what's possible when you combine salvaged materials with curiosity and imagination.

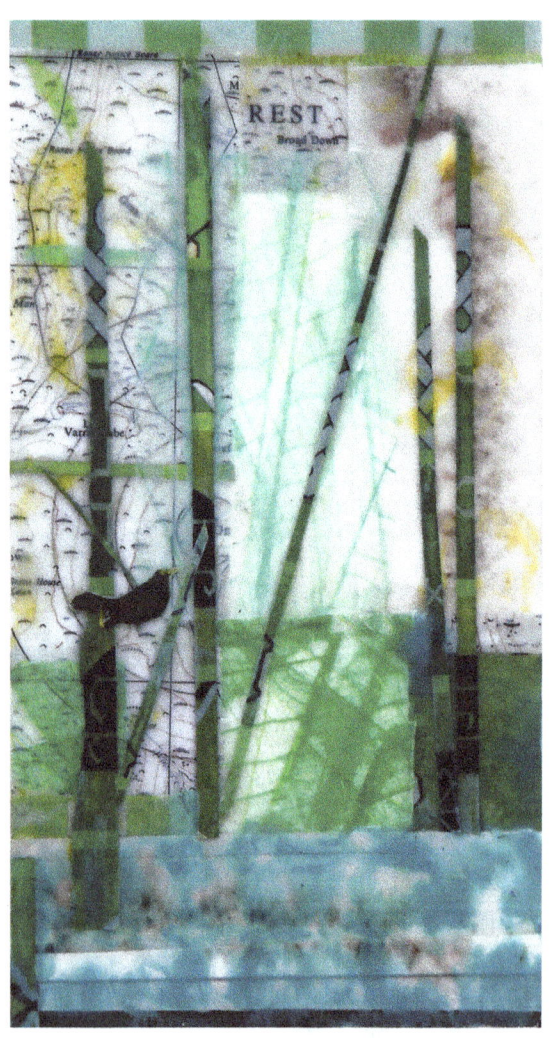

This piece has the same cellophane Kleenex wrapper in it that I used for the piece on page 120. It can be seen clearly in the top center of the piece. The bottom background was a molded page from a book that did not survive a flood at Hollins' Library. On top, I modeled blue dripped wax with a flat brush not trying to cover the whole surface so the pages peek through.

   The tree-like structures are thin strips of a magazine page. I use a Fiskar paper cutter a lot to cut strips of magazine pages to use like paints. The left side background is a map.

   The top is a strip of scrapbook paper and the left side background is handmade monotype paper. There is only one coat of clear wax medium except for the blue modeling at the bottom.

The entirety of this piece is made up of various papers such as scrapbooking paper, wallpaper and magazine pages. They are glued directly to the substrate. Next, one coat of clear wax medium was applied and while it was still warm I pressed a small leaf cookie cutter into the wax and removed immediately. I filled in the grooves with black oil paint stick and wiped off the surface with canola oil. There is one final clear wax medium coat and fusing to finish.

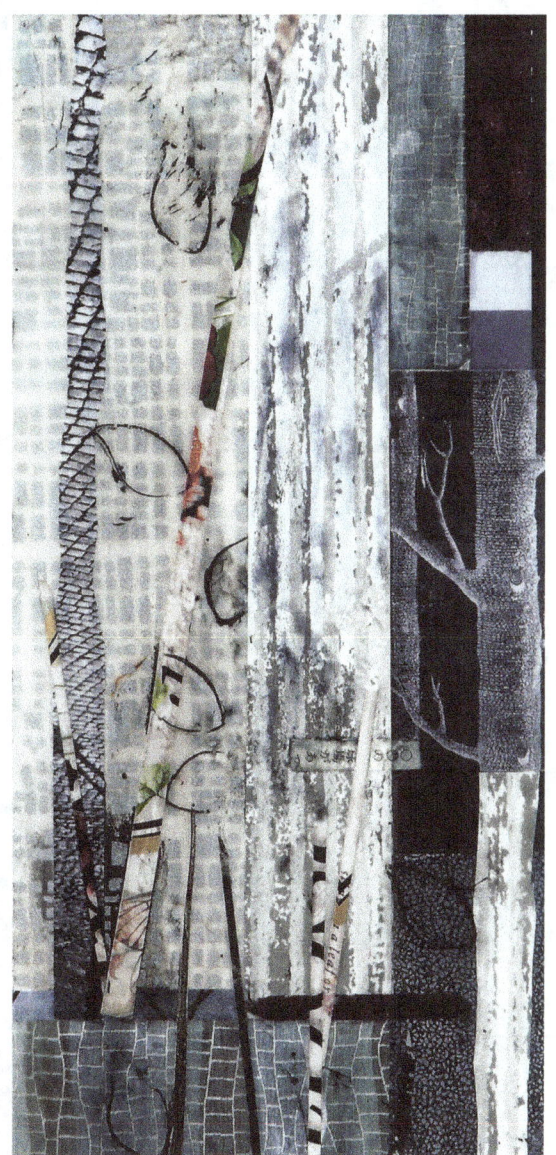

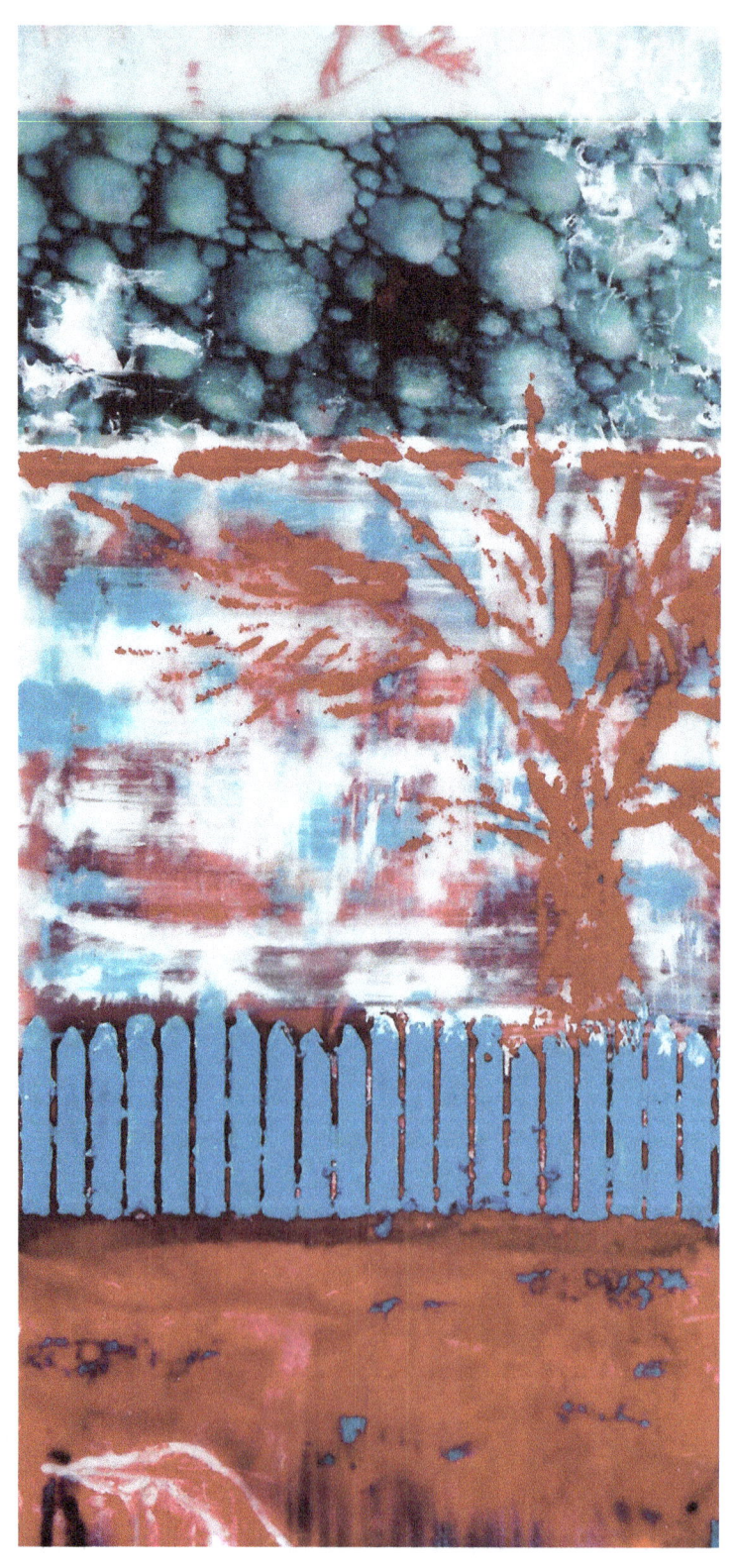

A portion of a larger piece and an example of pigmented wax modeling. The thin top strip was done with a razor blade at an angle. The blue circles below it are a color photocopy from a magazine page and it is Iguana skin under a microscope. There is some opaque white wax modeled and dripped onto the right side and left to carry the color white around.

The middle section with the red tree has a background that was painted with white, then blue, then red. I used a razor blade at an angle to model the surface. Next I used a flat brush edge dipped into red opaque wax and with dozens of marks, drew a tree.

The blue fence was done with a stencil of plastic that came in a perfume box as part of the packing. I used it like a stencil with several swipes of the flat side of a brush, building up the wax off the surface. When slightly cool I lifted the stencil carefully.

The bottom was painted in a layer of white, then red, then blue. Most of the blue I scraped off with the razor blade. The white is the head of a bird. I used a sharp tool to incise a drawing of a bird, then used white pastel in the grooves. I cleaned with canola oil, and topped with one coat of clear wax medium and fused.

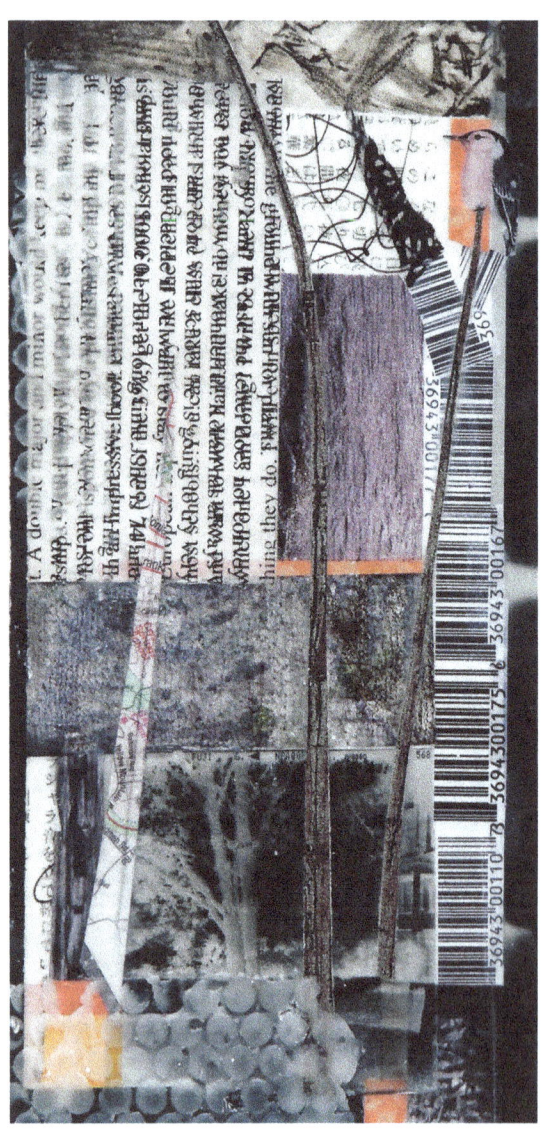

Here, various interesting papers were glued directly to the substrate. They include a piece of a map, Asian writing from an old book, two of my diary pages accidentally printed on top of each other, and a strip of barcodes fashioned into a tree, mimic trees and bark. There is one photo negative in the middle of a tree. Care must be taken when fusing a negative because, like cellophane, it tends to curl at the edges if it is overheated. Apply wax carefully. A little thicker wax around the edges helps, and fuse ever so lightly.

One coat of clear wax medium is over the entire piece and then fused. At the bottom is a strip of stenciling done with packing material in clear wax medium with several brush swipes of clear wax. Then, the work is barely fused so as not to disturb it too much.

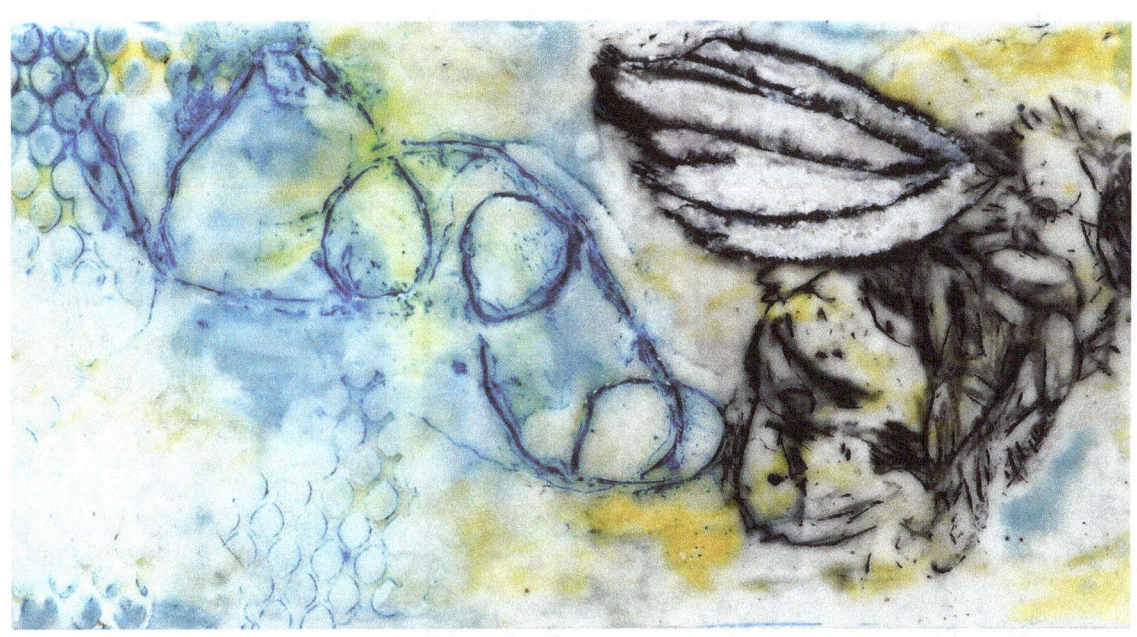

This is an example of sgraffito, and stenciling. The background is dribbled blue and yellow pigmented sheer wax. I was not trying to cover the entire substrate however. There is an underlying drawing of a bee on the right in the first layer of wax. Then two layers of wax over top of the drawing in which I used a sharp tool to incise the lines of the bee's body but not the lines of the entire drawing. I then filled in the grooves with black oil paint stick and wiped it clean with canola oil on the surface. You can still see some of the drawing deep down which makes the bee appear fuzzy. I filled in the wings with Hylla Evan's pearlized white pigmented wax.

I then incised lines to show the bee's flight pattern and filled in the grooves with as dark blue oil wax stick. When cleaning I chose to leave some residue on the surface and in the edges of the built up wax to the left which was done with a packing material stencil. One coat of clear wax medium was applied over the entire piece and fused.

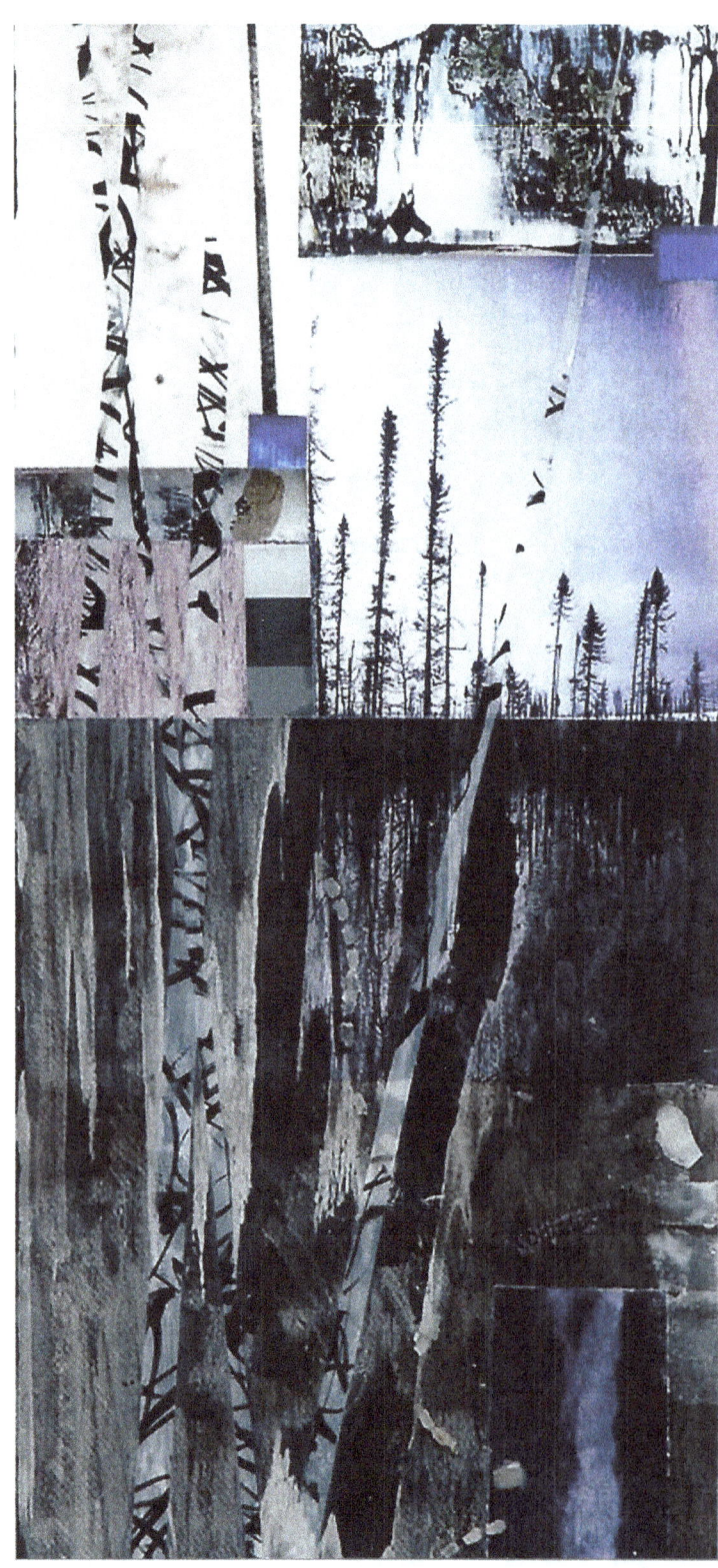

A detail from a larger piece done with various papers mimicking trees and bark. It has one actual magazine photo of pine trees on the right. The top right is hand-colored paper. Some of the surface trees are made from strips of velum with black permanent ink markings on them; a "trash find". This piece has one coat of clear wax medium on the surface.

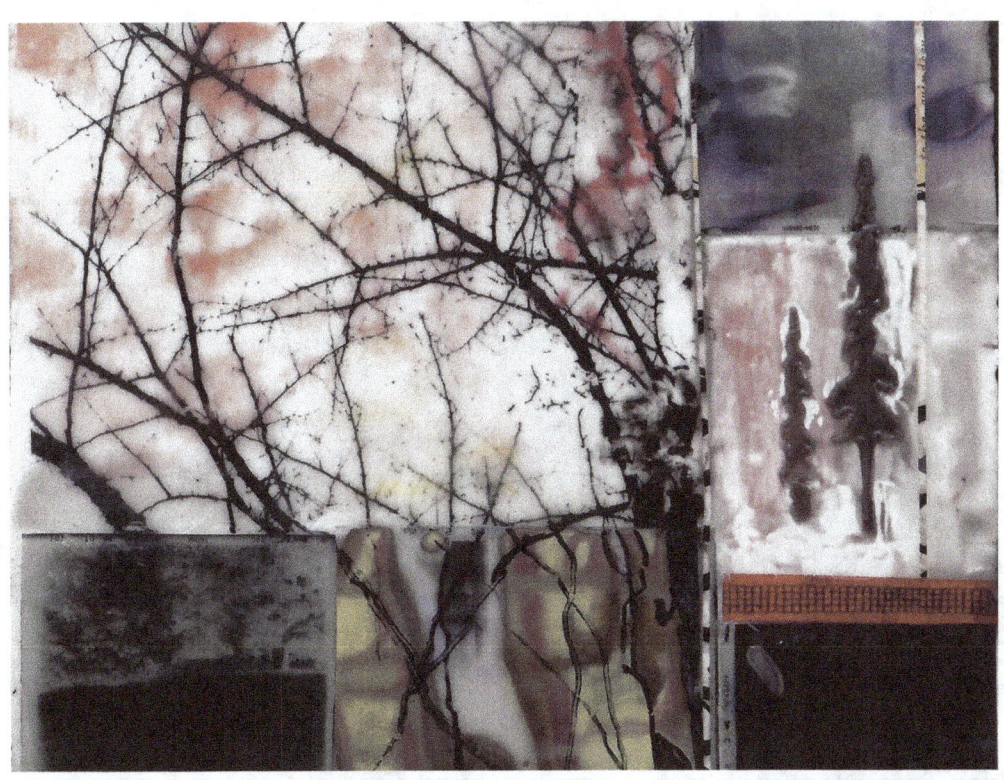

Here, the entire bottom and top right-hand corner is made of photo negatives. The one on the right is clearly taken of trees. The others have had obvious emulsion problems that make interesting patterns. I have drawn lines in black permanent marker on top of some connecting the lines of tree branches. On the far right center are two stenciled trees in grey wax. I used a brass embossing stencil to build up the wax. The top left is painted and fused wax in red-pinks and yellow. I did not try to cover the entire white substrate. I used a transfer method and a black-and-white photocopy for the trees over the top of the pink and yellow background. I then applied one clear coat of wax medium over the entire surface and fused.

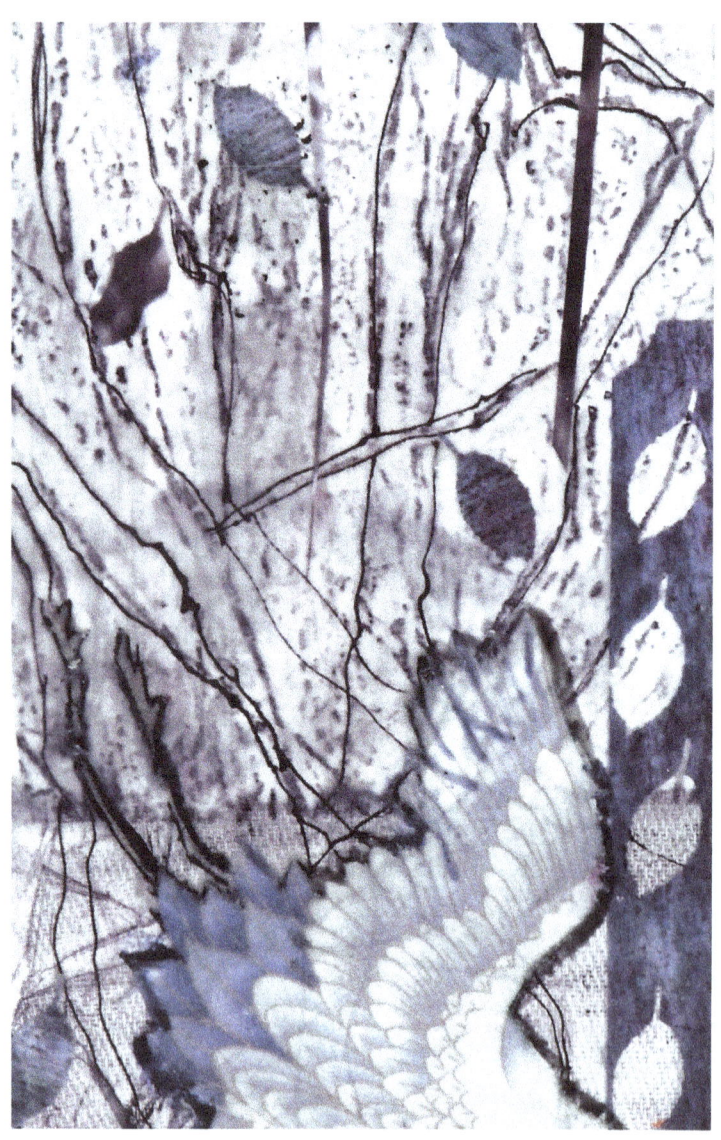

A paper-towel-background is a great place to start a piece! I glued it with a glue stick directly to the substrate. The crane—a fabric cutout—glued to the paper towel. The scattered leaves are punched out of wallpaper and the negative is to the right. It shows the paper towel underneath. I have drawn on the surface with a black permanent marker to make connections and outline the crane. One coat of clear wax medium is over the surface and then fused.

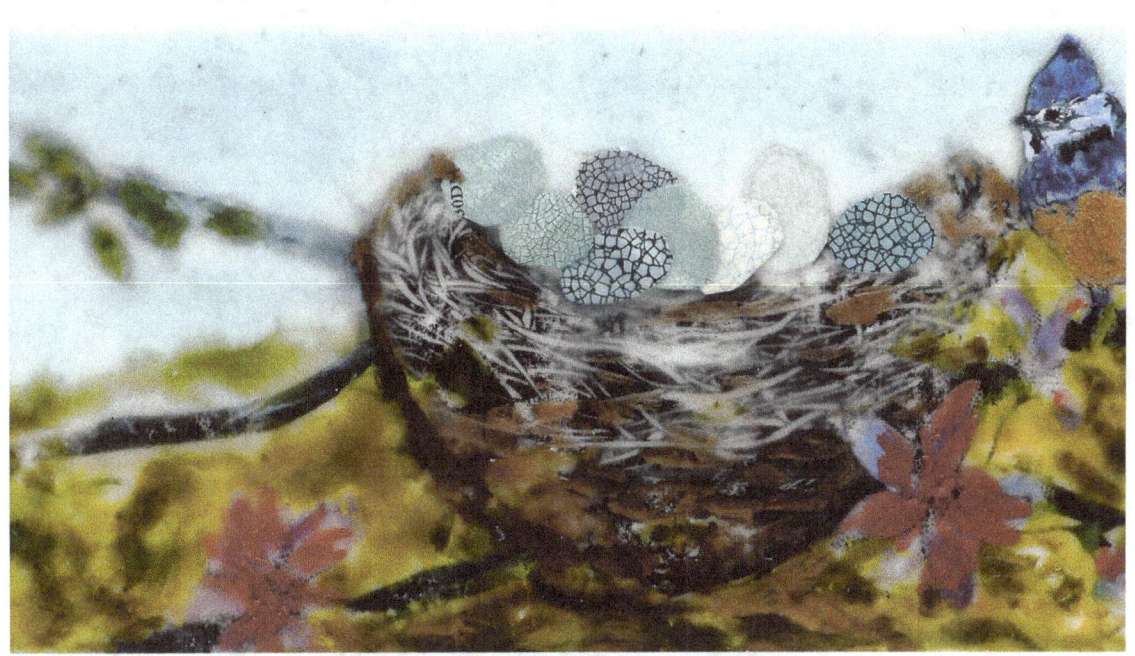

I used here a background of light blue wax and mottled tan-yellow wax at the bottom. I did not try to cover all of the substrate on the bottom but did on the top. The nest is a black-and-white photocopy of a magazine article transferred onto the wax surface. I then painted brown wax on with a fine brush on certain parts of the nest. The eggs were hand-cut out of paper paint sample chips. The bird is drawn entirely with a fine brush and wax. The flowers are also drawn and modeled with rose-colored wax. One coat of clear wax medium is on the top and fused.

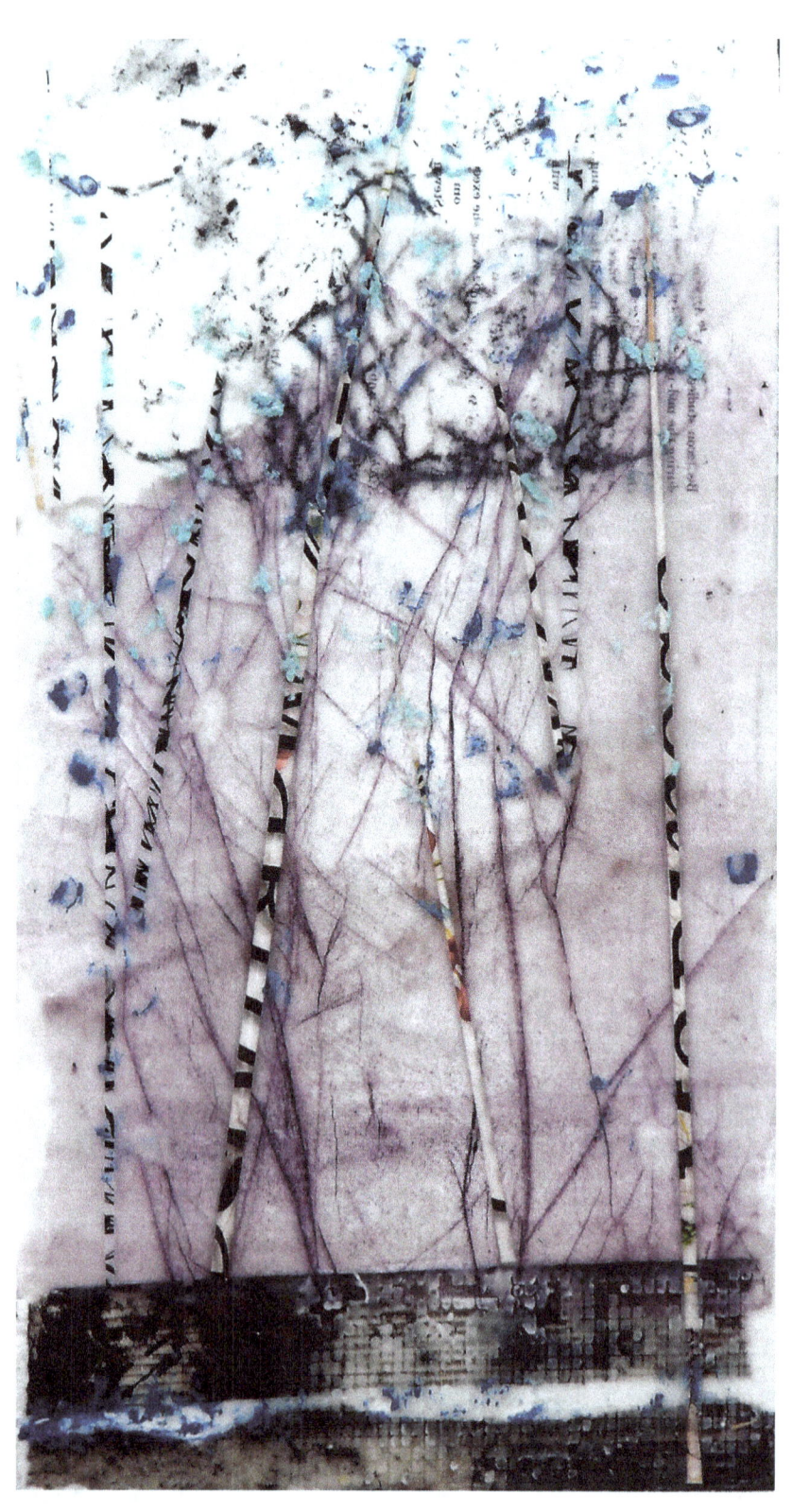

This is one of my favorites and also was Professor Dahlstrom's favorite. It became a gift to her for a wonderful semester. It begins with a paper towel, inked with a brayer and glued directly to the substrate. Thin strips of paper with black marks came from the light cardboard packaging pieces of what was inside of a scrapbooking paper stack. They look like birch trees, yes?

The bottom background is white pages used to wipe ink from etching plates, glued to the substrate. Over top of it are several swipes of clear applied over yellow dry wall tape used as a stencil.

The top has a transfer using a black-and-white mirror image copy of a book page. One coat of wax was applied over on top of the transfer and it was then over fused so some of the words wandered to the left.

The last to go on were dark blue and light teal blue pastels daubed on to mimic leaves. One coat of clear wax medium went on the entire surface and was then fused.

150

LATER LAYERS

Making art continues for me though I'm a different person now than I was when I first took control of my journey as an artist all those years ago after retiring from my work as a hair stylist. The art has changed me. This final section shares some of the work I completed after finishing my formal art eduction.

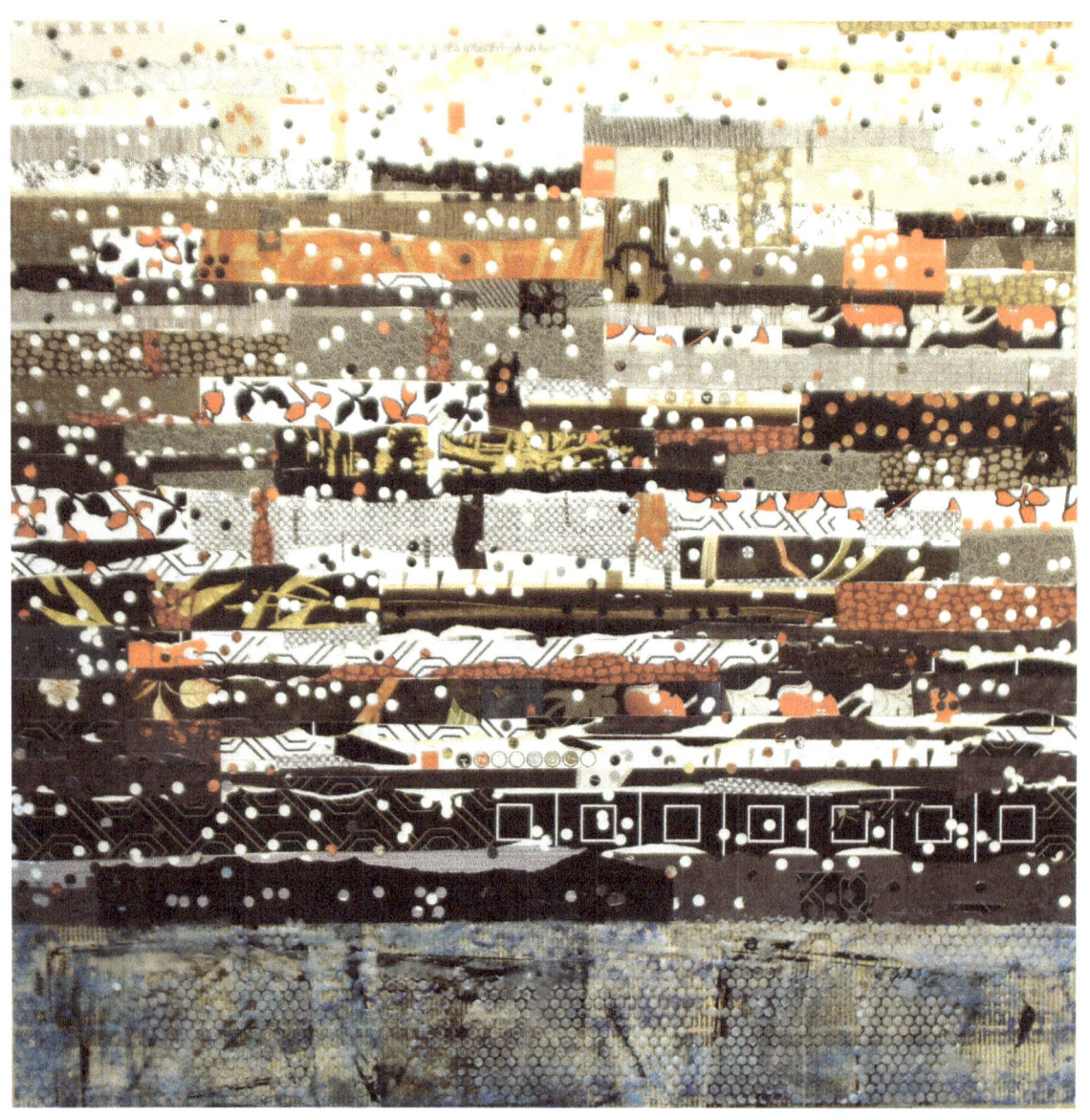

This piece came to me in a dream and is a part of what I describe as my lasagna series. The bottom background is white telephone book pages that I used to clean off black oil printmaking ink from the brayer. The patterns were interesting to me so I kept them and they wanted to live in this piece.

Over it, I used packing material as a stencil and built up wax, then caught the edges of the wax with a blue oil stick. The rest is pieces of wallpaper. I first slice out the wallpaper from its book with a razor blade and sort it into color piles for future use. What is left is an inch or so in the binder with heavy staples holding it between heavy cardboard. Getting the staples out is no small feat! But I can not bear to thrown it away. I spend hours trying to salvage it. It has holes in the paper where the staples were so I use a small hole punch to tidy up the holes then randomly punch out areas in the rest of the strip. Then I wonder what to do with the little paper circles. They want to live there also, so I carry the colors around, pasting them on the top of the wallpapers.

I had been reading a spiritual book on the power of intent and this piece reflects how we all have intent percolating up within us. We all have the power to do good things or bad. When the intent is to do good, I feel we are aligned with the Universe and we are helped.

Slowly Sifting Up from the Pool of Intent 2
Encaustic wax collage on wood panel
24" × 24" (61cm × 61cm)
Published in Incite 4: The Best of Mixed Media *edited by Tonia Jenny*

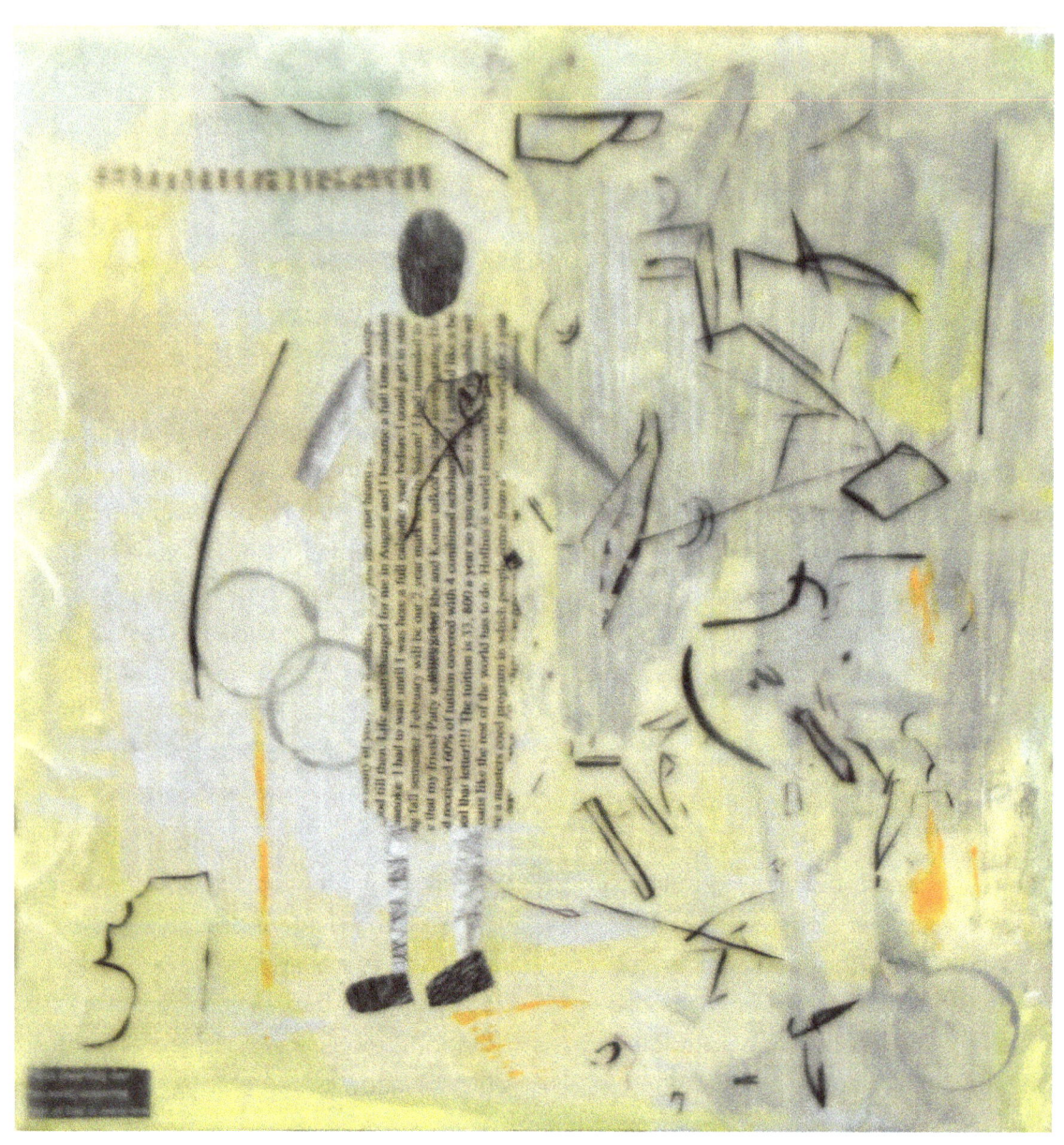

Broken
Encaustic wax collage on wood panel
12" × 12" (30cm × 30cm)

This piece is a self portrait. It reflects how I have viewed myself for most of my life until I finished school at fifty three.

One of my Horizon classmates was doing a print of a train. She had traced it on Mylar with a black sharpie and when she cut it out was not so precise about cutting inside the lines. She had a little pile of the clippings on the table and I asked her "What are ya gonna do with that?" pointing to the pile. She replied, "Trash." I happily scooped them up as treasure. I have since purposefully recreated the not-so precise cutting for other pieces of artwork, loving the look.

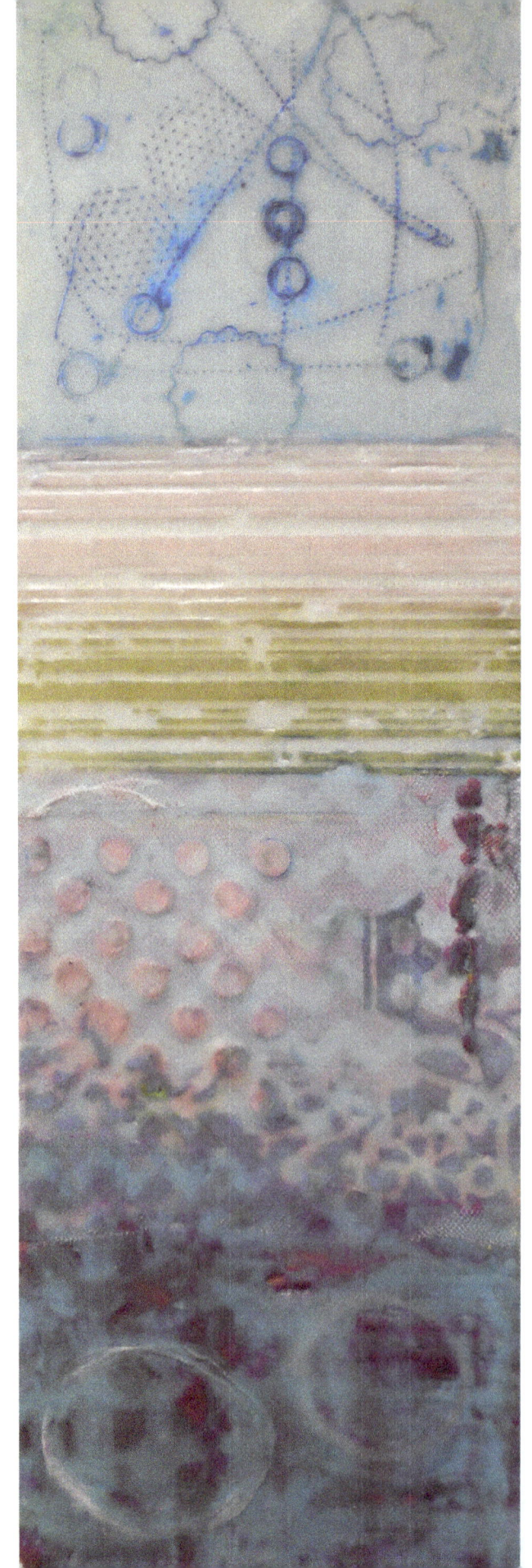

This is a demonstration piece done at the Fincastle open studios tour, so there is not a title. My professor invited me to be a guest artist not long after I graduated.

   I set up on her deck and showed people the process of encaustics. I used stencils to build up the wax on the surface and a sewing tool to draw into the wax. I then embedded paper with circles.

   I see a future body of work leaping from this piece. And, just like the potential that's pregnant in this work, I, too, am pregnant with the potential of discovering new layers to my art journey.

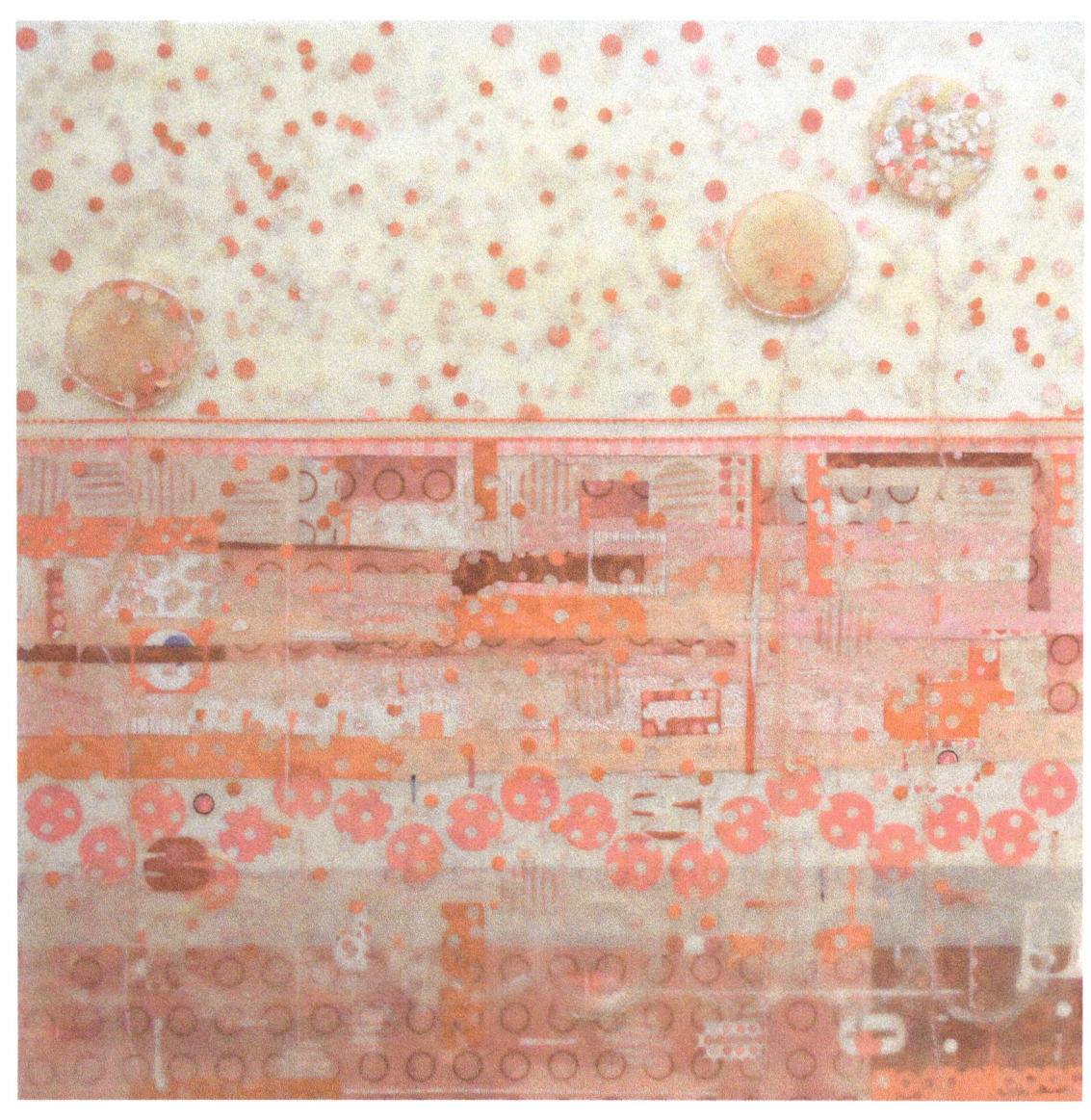

Three Balloons
Encaustic wax collage on wood panel
24" × 24" (61cm × 61cm)

"Three Balloons" was a gift to that broken little girl inside me who remembers vividly the first time she ever saw balloons at five-years of age. It was the only vacation day my mother ever took. We went with my Aunnie to Lakeside Amusement park fifty miles from where we lived.

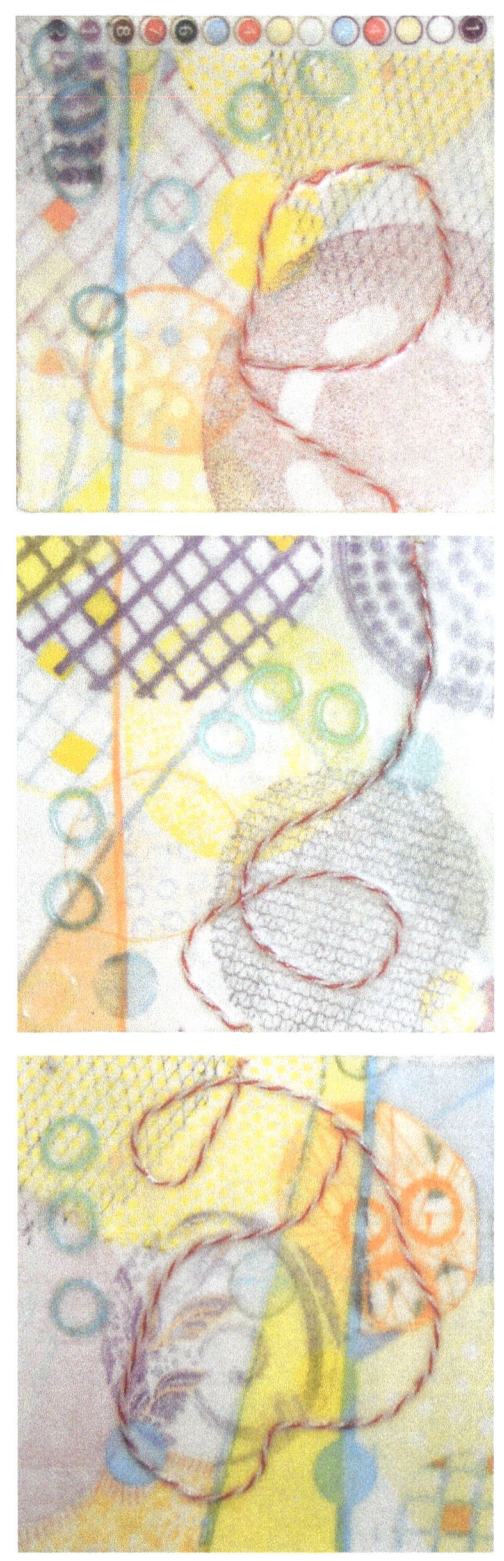

This was an experiment with 2"- (5cm-) deep canvas. I cut up old monotypes and glued to the canvas, then embedded string and colored hair rubber bands into the wax. If you look closely you will see the imprint of a tired band sander pad that I used to make the large circle mark in the bottom piece of the original monotype—a trash find. There is one coat of wax on the surface much the same way photographers use encaustic on their photographs. It meant I could salvage an unsuccessful monoprint and add another layer of interest on the surface.

   No titles as they are demo pieces. This was my first workshop of sorts three years after I graduated. Another four years later after nearly dying from a health scare, I would at last get back to making art.

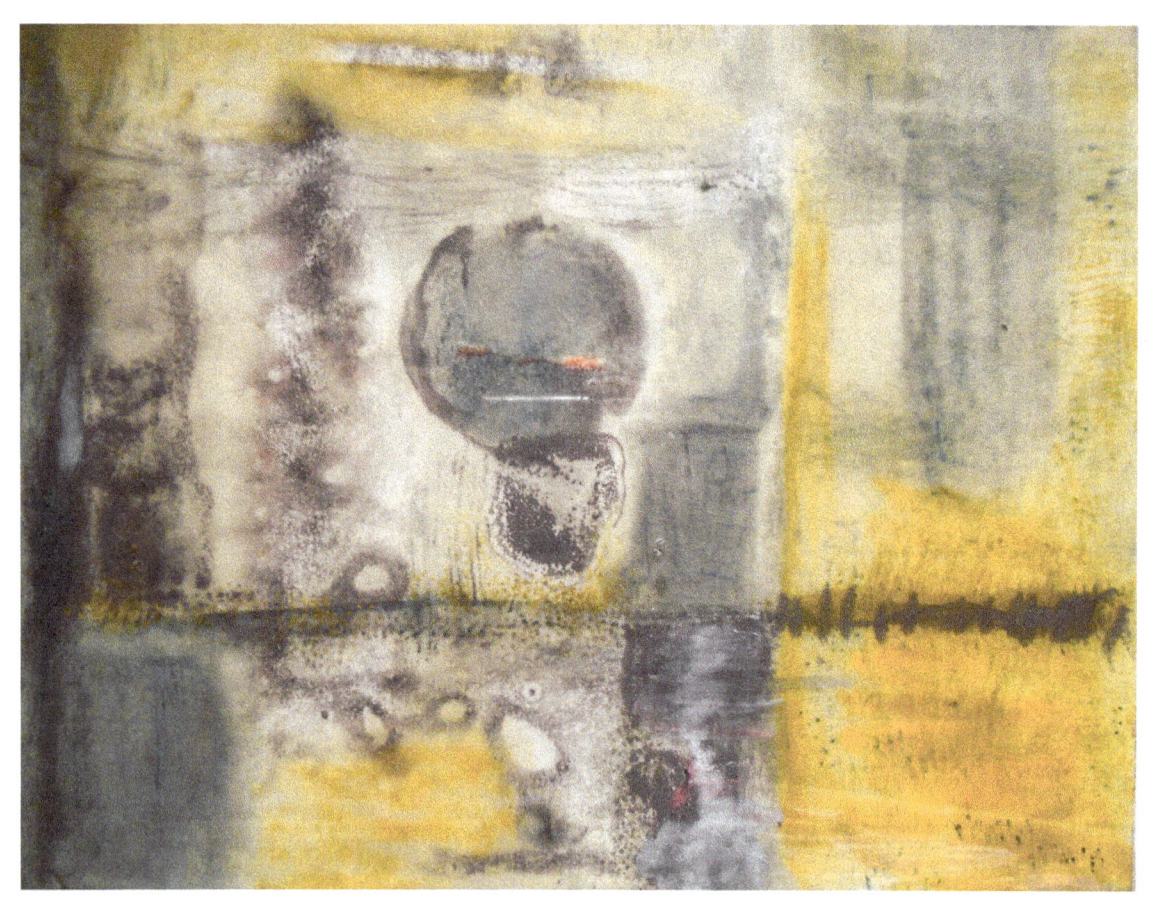

Sunset
Encaustic wax Monotype on Japanese Kozo paper
11" × 12" (28cm × 30cm)

This is an example of drawing on the paper with a wax stick while the paper is on a hot plate.

In a set of encaustic wax monotypes, I explored the future verses looking back to the past, using doors and windows as symbols. I was dealing with health issues and apprehensive about what the future would hold after I finished my studies.

AN EKPHRASTIC POEM
The Boating Party

By: Sharon Mirtaheri

Ahhhh sweet Renoir!
The intense talent that drives your hand,
agile, steady and sure of purpose.
Each fleck of paint
building on reality.
Slightest perceptions of light
brings sweating grapes,
shimmering crystal
to life.

I can hear the chatter
of contemplative reverie,
voices debating
politics and social issues,
vogue fashion
of the day.
Methodical lapping of water,
saltiness perfuming air,
against rocking boat;
accompaniment to intimate conversation.
I hear

tinkling laughter and giggles from women
amused by male flirtations and flattery.

Your strokes convey the mellowness
brought by flowing crimson wine
taking all my cares away
as I drown in your canvas.
A river of contentedness
making speaking gentlemen
more interesting,
sharpening my ears
to what he has to say.

I taste the warm buttery piquant cheese
as it coats my palate,
tart sweet ripeness of grapes.
Wine and companionship
makes the pinching of my corset,
the heat of layered clothing
sweat trickling down my spine,
bearable.

I can feel the texture
of clothes,
persimmon and sunflower yellow
draped on bodies,
Starched lace prickles my neck.
Brightly colored hats worn on heads
adorned with ribbon and silk flowers.

I am in the presence of great talent,
artists and writers,
extreme thinkers of our day.
How deft your hand,
how true your sight,
Oh Renoir…
To make this scene
Come to life!

Note: An ekphrastic poem is a poem written about a specific piece of artwork.

CONCLUSION

Life for everyone is really a roller-coaster ride of ups and downs. During my last class for my Master's degree, I needed an emergency appendectomy. Complications following my surgery derailed intentions of finishing a three-book memoir for my thesis, and I ended up doing an art thesis in encaustic wax collage instead, as it was easier and more enjoyable. I was not well for a year. I had to get a job to pay off my school loans and no one would hire a fifty-four year old for the jobs I was applying for, so I went back to doing hair. My health continued to decline but I finished the thesis.

In 2015, I ended up in a mental ward after trying to take my own life due to the horrible pain I was in. I had a headache daily for two years that often turned into a migraine, and that for which no pain killer—not even morphine—would get rid of.

My entire body ached like I had been in a car accident. When I was released, I sought out an osteopathic doctor who knew right off that I had Hashimoto's autoimmune disease as I had every symptom and I likely had had it for ten years. My primary care doctor and two endocrinologists—all allopathic doctors—let me fall through the cracks and nearly die. We would find out later I also had Lyme disease (old and new infections) and Bartonella (cat scratch fever), tic borne co-infection, and Epstein-Barr virus. Most of my nutrients were in emergency status, especially B12. You can die from any of those if untreated and I definitely was close to dying and not of my own doing.

It's hard to not remain angry about the fact that my doctor kept telling me it was "just menopause."

I had to give up being in the gallery, making art, cutting friends' hair, being primary caretaker of my beloved Aunnie, driving and being self-sufficient. My darling husband took care of me and continues to do so. I have clawed my way back to having a life!

After nearly seven years I am in remission and have my energy back and that wicked pain is gone. I am so blessed!

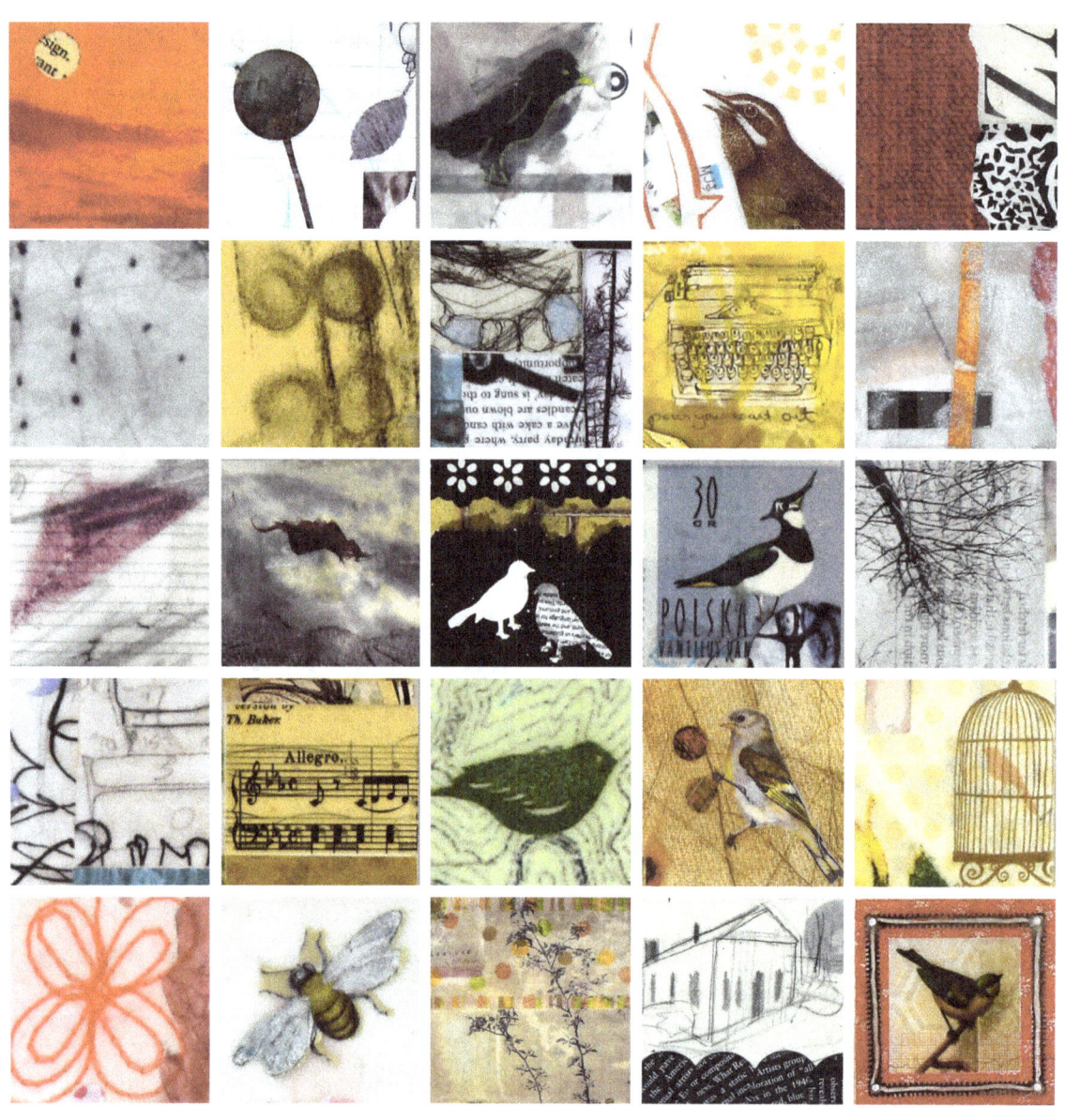

I love my life and still have a lot that I want to accomplish. I am in the garden nearly every day early-spring through late-fall and it is looking pretty fabulous, I must say.

I am making art again, mostly encaustics, but doing other creative things like making garden ornaments as focal points with glass dishes and salvaged metals that I paint. And, after having the materials for over twenty years, but never having had the time, I finally got around to making fabric Christmas trees and ribbon wreaths to give to friends last year during the lock down.

I am nearly finished with the first book of my memoir. The goal of giving proceeds from it to the Battered Women's Shelter at the Rescue Mission keeps me inspired to finish it. I'd love to hold my first book signing there as I truly want it to be a book of inspiration—especially for women in abusive situations—that they, too, can change their lives. If I can go to college at forty six, they can also.

I want women to reach for their dreams. Because dreams can come true. "Gift" yourself your dreams.

In conclusion, sometimes my work is described as decorative—usually the kiss of death in the art world. Whether it is decorative craft or art, I leave to others to decide; it makes no difference to me.

My focus is on the journey of being creative and pushing in that direction. I have discovered the best way to get to know one's own soul is through the creative process. I have found my voice and I choose to sing a song of joy for nature's blessings.

RESOURCES

Supplies

Ampersand Art Supply (substrates)
ampersandart.com

Dick Blick (brushes, oil sticks, substrates)
dickblick.com

Daniel Smith (brushes, oil sticks, substrates)
danielsmith.com

Enkaustikos (educational site and great tools)
fineartstore.com

Evans Encaustics (purist, most densely-pigmented waxes)
evansencaustics.com

Gamblin Paints (safety information)
gamblincolors.com

Kremer Pigments (powered pigments)
kremer-pigmente.com

Miles Conrad Encaustics (custom paint blends)
custom-encaustics.com

R&F Paints (educational videos and safety info)
rfpaints.com

Sinopa (powdered pigments
sinopa.com

Wagner Encaustics, Inc.
elisewagner.com/Wagner-encaustics

Encaustic Wax Organizations

Fused Wax Chicago
fusedwaxchicago.org

International Encaustics Artists
international-encaustics-artists.org

New England Wax
newenglandwax.org

Southern Arizona Chapter of the IEA
sazwax.wordpress.com

South Eastern Encaustic Artists
southeasternartistscom

Texas Wax
texaswaxdallas.blogspot.com

Google "Encaustic Wax Conference" on information on upcoming and past educational conferences.

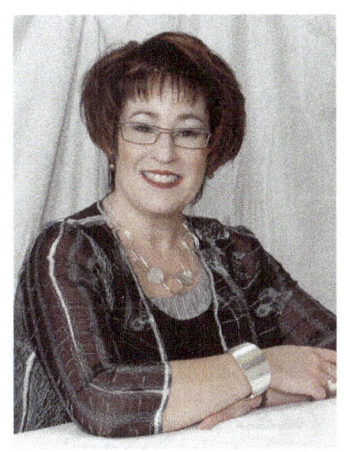

Sharon Mirtaheri

At 62, I have a long list of things I want to accomplish with the rest of my life, given good health. I would love to learn to play the piano and to sew. I would like to see the gardens of the world—especially Monet's garden in France and Butchart Gardens in Victoria BC.

I want to give back to the world; to help others—especially women—traverse to the same great place in which I have found myself: happy being creative.

I hope to finish my three-book memoir and do a book signing tour when the pandemic is over. I want to get back to volunteering at my local rescue mission but not cutting hair this time. I have some ideas of working with women in the Battered Women's shelter, doing a body of artwork that includes solar plate etchings of photographs of their childhoods and including their life narratives. It would be a traveling art show for public spaces like libraries and could make a strong statement against domestic violence.

I have a vision for a stream of revenue for the mission involving sales of a biscotti product, such as Paul Newman did with his products. I see in my mind, trucks with Angel Biscotti delivering all over the valley to hair salons. I did a cost analysis of this idea when I had an internship with the mission as a January term project at Hollins.

I have always thought "Angels with Scissors" could be a national organization. The idea of hairstylists all over the country organized and volunteering in rescue missions and shelters, lives in my soul. It would be a huge undertaking but would make a huge impact.

I have never been one to sit still very long. You can follow my journey on my website and my profile on Facebook, where you can also find additional information on encaustic wax.

It's never too late to have a happy childhood!

www.sharonmirtaheriart.com

Copyright © 2021 by Sharon Mirtaheri

All rights reserved. Without the prior written permission of the author, no part of this publication may be reproduced, stored, distributed, or transmitted in any form or by any means, including photocopying, recording, scanning, electronic, mechanical methods, or otherwise, except as permitted under Section 107 or 108 of the 1976 United States Copyright Act, in the case of brief quotations embodied in reviews and certain other non-commercial uses permitted by copyright law. Requests to the author and publisher for permission should be addressed to theshasha1@gmail.com.

Printed in the United States of America

First Printing, 2021

ISBN-13: 978-1-7376963-0-8 (Paperback edition)

Editor and designer: Tonia Jenny www.toniajenny.com

Published by Sharon Mirtaheri

www.sharonmirtaheriart.com

www.ingramcontent.com/pod-product-compliance
Lightning Source LLC
Chambersburg PA
CBHW082247220526
45469CB00009B/2909